Quilt of Many Colors

Quilt
of Many
Colors

A Collage of Prose and Poetry

by

Grayce Bonham Confer

Beacon Hill Press of Kansas City
Kansas City, Missouri

ISBN: 083-411-3589

Printed in the
United States of America

Cover: Crandall Vail

10   9   8   7   6   5   4   3   2   1

This book is lovingly dedicated to:

> Lt. Col. Ethel C. Naffah, Ret., and
> Lt. Comdr. Ned Naffah, Ret.—
> > Lifelong kin, very friends.

> Also
> Drs. Rol and Eileen Lucas and
> Art and Del Benkert—
> > Lifelong friends, almost kin.

Contents

Foreword

Quilt of Many Colors is a lively collage that witnesses to Grayce Bonham Confer's faith in the beauty and ultimate triumph of the human spirit and in the importance of such enduring virtues as love, patience, courage, honesty, industry, and trust. It begins with an account of her initial effort to find a publisher as well as readers with whom to share her work. It is a narrative involving rejection (her husband, Harold, didn't think she would find a receptive publisher) and acceptance (a publisher responded favorably and with a stipend, and her husband became her primary supporter). The poems and stories in *Quilt* reflect the values and faith that have permeated and sustained the lives of Grayce and Harold Confer. Rejection and wounds both psychological and physical require reconciliation and healing. Life is not easy. Sometimes it is nearly more than an aching heart can bear, but the human spirit finds a way of enduring and transcending the unsatisfactory and painful aspects of existence through hard work, patience, honesty, long-suffering, loving, and being loved. Christian virtues, the virtues of faith, hope, and love, are a common thread throughout the book, especially love of family, love of God, and love of neighbor (the latter as understood by the Confers includes all of God's children).

I am grateful for the opportunity to provide a foreword to Grayce's *Quilt,* for as a friend of her family and longtime colleague of her beloved and now deceased husband, I have been privileged to play a small part in her life.

Harold Confer was one of my spiritual mentors; within the context of his church, he introduced me to many writings and music that have touched my life. Later I was privileged to join him as a colleague on the faculty at San Bernardino Valley College. In the context of my interaction with Harold, I met Grayce, their son, Harold, Jr., and their daughter, Viletta. My life has been blessed by each of them.

—DR. ROGER SCHMIDT
Redlands, Calif.

Preface
(about quilts)

A quilt is a form of art. Our first visual response to viewing a coverlet is the color and the design or pattern. The small pieces, usually hand-sewn together, express an idea in the blending of abstract colors or the developing of a structured motif. Early quilts used odd-shaped, free-form bits of cloth, producing what was termed a "crazy" quilt. Our ancestors lived by the adage "Waste not, want not," and that included using every scrap of material for those needed covers. Artists (quilters) create a landscape upon which march a history of many people, in many situations. Which leads me to my next premise.

A quilt is a welding of history. Often those small wisps of material mirror an entire family's life, even crossing back several generations. That very dark brown is a snip from Great-grandmother's floor-length skirt shown in that tintype; here is a piece of Grandmother's alpaca purple wedding dress; those solid and striped materials represent the many shirts, nightshirts, and even underdrawers Grandma made for her menfolk. Those rainbow colors from the dresses of several generations of females intermingle in the quilt as they did in life. So a quilt is a metaphor of life itself, past and present.

Finally, quilts are a form of communication. Two of my sisters and I lingered over a quilt made by our mother, recalling dresses from certain events, years, and people from a shared past. My own daughter appreciated learning of *her* past through the pieces from our mother's needlework. So we realize that quilts are a true art form of communication, turning back a page or two of recorded history. The human spirit, frail or robust, is eternal.

Please turn back a corner of my *Quilt*. The varicolored pieces have been combined with loving care, representing many types of persons, placed in a variety of settings. Some of my "blocks" are true, some fictionalized fact, others plain fiction. A few of my "scraps of material" have seen print; most have not. Indeed, a "crazy" quilt!

Despite the changing backgrounds and odd-shaped pieces in my *Quilt of Many Colors,* the overriding pattern is the emergence of the human spirit into a warm covering of comfort, inspiration, reassurance, understanding, forgiveness, love, and togetherness.

To repeat, the human spirit is eternal.

In Appreciation

To the *Family* magazine, *Negro Digest, Scriblerus, Light and Life, The Standard, The Banner, Soundings, Plymouth Village Crier,* the *Facts* newspaper, and the *World of Poetry Anthology* for having published some of the stories/articles/poetry included in this book.

"Moments of Decision," an imaginative soaring, would never have evolved without the professional suggestions from my sister-in-law, Ethel C. Naffah, a retired lieutenant colonel from the U.S. Air Force.

And to Ann Schmidt for her marvelous computer art, added to her gracious willingness.

We Are Our Words

One word does not a book make,
But one word followed by many others
Becomes a sentence, a paragraph, a page—
At long last, a book.

We read: "In the beginning was the Word,"*
And "Thy word is a lamp unto my feet."**
Then words are painted as "wise," "true,"
"Magnified," having comfort and joy.***
So today we give thanks for words:
   Those that identify, those that clarify,
   The ones that illustrate, that paint us beauty;
   Words that sing, the ones that laugh,
   That cry with us and lift our spirits,
   Words to lead, encourage, and bless,
   That open the door to new friends
   While endearing more closely the old ones.

We are known by our words, so
Speak carefully, and in truth.
One word does not a book make.
Yet we are our words and our lives a book.

*John 1:1.
**Ps. 119:105.
***Pss. 19:7; 119:160; 138:2; Jer. 15:16.

My Turning Point as a Writer

A friend, reading some of my yellowed manuscripts, exclaimed, "I can't believe you've never tried selling any of these! Why don't you take that marketing class at the college?"

With trepidation, I enrolled and learned how to prepare and submit a manuscript, how to "query," what SASE meant. In time, I completed two short stories I thought "pretty good" and read them to my professor-husband whose fine mind I respect. Wide-eyed and expectant, I awaited his verbal blessing, but my spirits sank as he gently said, "Darling, those are nice little stories and very well-written, but I doubt any magazine would pay money for them."

"You think they aren't good enough—right?"

"Well," he hedged. "I don't want you to be disappointed. Frankly, I can't visualize them in print."

He patted me apologetically as I tucked the pages away with other scribblings. After musing a few days, my rebellious nature asserted, "You'll never know until you try!"

So away flew the two nice little stories, and I began shuffling eagerly through the mail each day. One morning I spied a long envelope from that magazine. Nervously I expected a rejection, but both stories had been accepted! The accompanying check was proof!

Running to the phone, I dialed the college where my husband taught and was told he was in class. Calmly I said, "This is an emergency. Please call him to the phone."

My husband answered, his voice concerned. "What has happened?"

For a moment I felt ashamed, but only for a moment.

Sweetly I replied, "The most exciting thing has happened! I just received a long blue check for those little stories you said no publisher would buy . . ."

There was a long silence. "You mean that you called me from class just to tell me that?"

"That's right, Darling. Now you'll have a bit more faith in this little homebody."

Well, he became my most ardent supporter and often regaled groups of friends about my "emergency" call. And those two little stories formed the nucleus of my book *Faith and Fried Potatoes.*

That episode was my turning point as a writer.

How Marian Anderson Blessed My Life

I have never been one to seek out celebrities. Somehow it didn't appeal to me to join a noisy throng in order to secure an autograph or to shake the hand of a famous person—except once. I still contemplate on the urging that propelled me backstage that night in Milwaukee in 1944.

My husband was teaching in Wauwatosa, Wis., and our budget was tautly stretched. When a neighbor asked me to be her guest at Marian Anderson's concert, I was thrilled. I love music and was grateful for this opportunity, as we hadn't been able to afford many concerts. But my husband duly pointed out a stumbling block to my acceptance.

Years earlier I had lost a child and had been advised that I would probably never have another. I had become pregnant, and the doctor circumscribed my every move, prohibiting me from stairs, crowds, high heels, and weariness. I desperately wanted this child, but I was determined to hear this wonderful woman, in person. So to my husband's arguments, I promised to be *careful, very careful!*

It was a joy to be in a crowded hall. People streamed in from every direction, some garbed in glamorous evening attire, while others were in casual street clothes.

The lights were dimmed, and a hush descended over the assemblage. The curtains parted to reveal a plain stage—empty but for a little man seated at a grand piano, and Miss Anderson herself. She stood tall and still, almost forbidding in her bearing.

Applause thundered throughout the vast building, and still she stood quietly, almost statuelike. There were no sweeping curtsies and sparkling smiles. Her somber eyes expressed interest as they swept over the upturned faces. When the ovation finally died away, she merely lowered her head in acknowledgment and signaled her accompanist to begin.

Time stood still for me as she sang. The purity of her voice reached out to embrace each person. I realized that this lady didn't need to resort to staged mannerisms or gestures. Her gift was her lovely instrument in which she gave unreservedly in a varied offering of classics, German lieder, and spirituals. She, alone, was the channel through which beauty flowed.

Encore followed encore until she finally sang Schubert's "Ave Maria." The attentive crowd was spellbound. As the last note faded away, a holy solemnity seemed to pervade the place. I mopped my wet cheeks and, glancing around, saw tears on other faces, both black and white. (This group was figuratively on its knees.) Gradually people arose until everyone was standing in silent tribute, and then they began filing out as if from a place of worship.

My neighbor and I had reached a side exit when I impulsively turned to her and said, "Ione, I must go backstage and tell Miss Anderson what inspiration and courage her singing has given me. I must tell her! Do you mind?"

She looked at me, then at her watch.

"Well-l-l, your husband *did* say not to be too late, you know."

"Yes, I know; but I've never felt so moved in my life! It won't take too much longer."

She smiled indulgently; after all, pregnant women often get extreme ideas!

"All right. I'll go along," she answered.

The line of greeters was longer than I had anticipated, and I shifted my uncomfortable weight from one swollen foot to the other. Ione looked more and more disapproving.

17

Slowly we approached the great lady, and I thought of the verbal bouquet I would present her.

When I finally stood before her, no words came. She was taller than I, and as she gazed down on my tent-shaped figure, her dark liquid eyes seemed to hold all the sadness and compassion in the world. Then her large, strong hand grasped mine, and my flowery words slipped from mind as I heard myself murmuring brokenly, "Oh—may God bless you!"

Onstage, she had only offered fragments of smiles, but now she suddenly flashed a wide one that lighted her face. Her reply remained with me like a benediction through the next difficult days: "Thank you! He will be blessing you, too, before long!"

And He did. Two weeks later, a lovely girl-child was born to us.

By rights, this story is finished, but an epilogue must be added to show how Miss Anderson inspired and encouraged me and later gave me comfort.

A very few years ago, my mother was in our home slowly dying from cancer. One Sunday night, Marian Anderson made a guest appearance on TV, and I turned up the volume so that her voice would reach Mama in the bedroom. When the warm, rich voice began singing "He's Got the Whole World in His Hands," I slipped to Mama's door to see how she liked it. I paused, unobserved, as I saw a bony hand upraised and heard Mama say with conviction, "And He's got *me* in His hands, too!"

The memory of that scene, etched indelibly on my mind, comforted me often after Mama died. Again, Marian Anderson had blessed my life.

A Mother's Lament

"Please, leave me alone!" I begged them all: the doctor with his sedatives, the well-meaning friends, even my husband. "Please . . ."

And so they filed out, puzzled, worried. But they need not worry. I shall not do anything drastic; I value life too much. It is just that I must have isolation in order to think. And now, after pacing around Darryl's room, I find myself in the attic, seated at my old desk, trying to put down some of my rambling thoughts. Oh, if I could only weep for my young son! But my eyes are dry.

This morning . . . was it only this morning? Yes, only a few hours ago that my son came running into our farm kitchen, books and wraps one jumble in his arms.

"Mom!" His voice shrilled in a noisy treble, then suddenly lowered several notes down the scale. "How's about a couple extra dollars for today? I really could use 'em and see . . . I brought an extra armload of wood for you." He nodded virtuously toward the overflowing woodbox.

"But Son, the week is only half gone, your allowance is *all* gone, and I've already given you money for your meals today while you're on the band trip. I think that's enough."

We are making payments on a farm and have two children in school. Nature and the milk check are not always dependable, so we are in the habit of counting every penny. It is the only way Jim and I have been able to slowly rise above a mountain of debt. So I felt justified in refusing Darryl the extra money even after he presented his final argument.

"But Mom! I wanted to ask Rosemary to go to the matinee with me at Madison, and now I can't and Chesty'll take her." His brown eyes were eloquent, but I answered self-righteously,

"My sakes! I don't know what you high school youngsters are coming to! Dates and more dates! Is that all you think about? Why, when I was your age—"

"Yeah, I know. You went to school to *study!* I'd sure like to know what fun you had if that's all you ever did!"

"Now, now, Son. No more argument. . . . Here, don't forget your cornet, and don't get into any mischief, and mind Mr. Smith . . ." All these admonitions were following the rushing figure, now halfway to the gate. Suddenly, remorse swept over me as I noticed how tall he was getting for his 15 years.

"Wait!" I called and ran to get my purse from the buffet drawer.

"Sentimental," my inner voice accused me. "Just spoiling him because you can't resist the way his hair falls over his eyes. Are you afraid he's growing away from you?"

But I sped down the lane after Darryl. As I reached him, all out of breath, and crushed the bills into his hand, his eyes lighted, and I saw that the tow hair he had so faithfully brushed close to his head was already escaping its confines. Impulsively, I yearned to gather him, books, cornet, and all close to my heart, but he'd never have forgiven me for embarrassing him before the other students.

"Hey, Mom!" He grinned widely. "You're OK. S'long!"

His changing voice came back to me as he swung onto the bus. I waved, and a dozen arms answered me.

I can't explain why I relived so much of Darryl's childhood during the day. Perhaps because he was our "baby," and the episode of the morning forced me to accept the fact he would soon be a young man. Eleanor is a freshman at the university, and not a day passes that I don't miss her; but today as I cooked and cleaned, my thoughts kept drifting to my son.

You probably would never have given my boy a second glance. He was a typical 15-year-old with freckled nose and wide, brown eyes that crinkled almost shut when he laughed. His clothes were the accepted sneakers and jeans, and he was beginning to voice opinions on many subjects of which he knew little; but we listened, remembering how we went through the period of trying on ideas for size. Honest, with occasional spurts of temper, he occasionally displayed moments of great gentleness.

I recalled the moment the nurse laid him in my arms; I was aghast at his skinny legs and large feet—Eleanor had been so fat! But the nurses reported what a good baby he was, and when I got him home, I learned they were right. He smiled early and developed such a big laugh that we made a record of it when he was only three months old. Tonight, I found that old, red disc wrapped carefully in one of his discarded flannelette diapers in a trunk.

Looking back, it seemed Darryl grew faster than Eleanor, cutting his teeth, walking and talking earlier. Each year flew faster than the one before. When he was eight, he disobeyed us and fished from the railroad trestle. When he saw the approaching train, he tumbled into the river below, and an older boy dragged him out, unhurt but scared. It was then that Jim taught Darryl to swim.

The things he collected! Pictures, maps, stamps, rocks, copper wire, and he would never permit me to throw anything away. Tonight, that chaotic assortment speaks volumes to me and helps to bring him close, for Darryl wasn't brought back to me—only the still, broken form of a boy who had been brimming with vitality, laughter, and noisy speech.

They said he had marched so proudly with the band. Just as proudly, he had taken Rosemary to the show and sat beside her on the bus during the happy ride home. After the bus stopped, he was crossing in front of it. Jim, waiting to

21

bring him home, saw the car that failed to stop, saw it zoom around the bus, heard the screech of brakes mingled with the shrill cries of children. Jim saw it all. No one else was hurt, only my Darryl is no more.

Dear God, how can a mother's heart swell and pain so without breaking? If I could only scream at the fate that is mine, or shed fountains of tears, or even slip into an insensible state! All I can feel now is a stupor, a numbness with the tight band across my chest and throat too dry to swallow. Dear God...

*   *   *

Hours later:

The sun is slowly rising as though uncertain of its welcome. Today is today; yesterday was yesterday. My son who was alive yesterday is dead today. But now I can bear my burden of grief, as hot tears stream from my weary eyes and sobs tear at my aching throat. Now I can weep at long last, and endure, remembering such a little thing. It was when I ran after Darryl to give him the extra money and he said,

"Hey, Mom! You're OK."

Ah, God, wonderful, healing tears ... as I can say, "Thanks for having our son for a season."

The Metamorphosis of Mrs. Doc

Mrs. Hammer was a dedicated young wife, endowed with efficiency, business acumen, and curly red hair that formed a soft halo around her face. At this moment, that face was stern. She remonstrated with her husband for the umpteenth time.

"But Tom, you're just too easy with your patients! Your profession demands more dignity—reserve. How can all these people respect you when you are *always* available, when you refuse to demand payment, when you let them call you 'Doc'? In a profession, business is business. And unless you are firm, your professional image will suffer! And you are a fine doctor," she finished with tears in her voice.

Dr. Hammer, a quiet man of 35, had been married 2 years to Kathryn, a former nurse who had been trained to observe protocol. She helped Tom in his office and despaired each time she tried to balance the books. There were entries of cash paid out for supplies and overhead, but the offsetting credits showed unusual entries, such as:

Grandma Lacey 2 chickens (=$2.00)

Peter Yankovich 4 days work in yard (=$16.00)

Miss Murple 1 crocheted tablecloth (=$12.00)

The doctor sighed, then replied, "I know this seems unbusinesslike to you, Dear, but I don't think it's unprofessional to be available. That is just part of my stock-in-trade, Kathryn, my Hippocratic oath, and if I'm not true to that, I'm not true to myself. For these people, Doc *is* a term of respect and affection. I can't squeeze blood from a turnip. If my families haven't money to pay for my services, they give what they *do* have. I'll never press them."

"They'd have to pay any other doctor, and you know it."

Kathryn set her pretty lips in a straight line. "That's one reason they call for you, because they know you are easy!"

"Now, Kathryn," Tom interrupted. (He wanted to call her Katy, but she felt it was undignified.) "I like to think people express confidence in me when they send for me."

"Well . . . yes," she conceded. "But no other doctor will go near that awful woman by the railroad tracks—that Miss Murple!"

Tom grinned. "Maybe they attend her in a different capacity! You'll have to admit she gave us a beautiful tablecloth. Why don't you ever use it?"

"The very thought revolts me, that's why!" Kathryn replied heatedly. "You just don't seem to understand, Tom. I'm trying to help you build a fine practice. At the rate you are going, you'll be plodding along in the same old car 20 years from now. You have to be businesslike in your profession to inspire confidence and respect."

Dr. Hammer sighed again. "You're probably right, Kathryn, and I'll try harder—I really will."

The phone rang shrilly, and Kathryn lifted the receiver, smiling warmly over the breakfast table at her husband. She felt a small sense of triumph.

"Dr. Hammer's residence," she acknowledged. "Yes, the doctor will be in his office in 30 minutes. I'll tell him to expect you."

Again she smiled as she relayed the message. It wasn't that she wanted more than what she felt was just compensation for her husband's time and services. She honestly felt the people of Glenfield took him for granted, expecting a lot for a little, not showing him earned deference. What did it matter that he had grown up here? He was now a fine doctor, and she was so proud of his capability.

"Doc is so common," she had often told him. "You are not, and neither is your profession!"

The doctor hadn't been able to convince her that 'Doc'

24

made him feel warm and accepted. So he simply ignored her habit of replying pointedly, "The doctor is in. Please be seated. The doctor will see you in about 20 minutes."

Kathryn was not rude. She was just polite.

The next morning Kathryn arose to an encompassing nausea. She tried to proceed with normal breakfast preparations but had to rush to the bathroom. Tom found her pale and shaken. To her horror he began to grin. "Mrs. Dr. Hammer, I think you are going to need the advice of a good physician for the next several months. I don't usually press my services, but in your case I'll make an exception!"

"Oh, no," Kathryn breathed. "We can't afford a baby yet!"

He led her into the bedroom and got a cold cloth for her forehead. "If everyone waited until they could afford a child, we wouldn't have to worry about population explosions! Personally, I'm tickled pink. You come in to the office later and let me make a test—just to be sure."

"But how will you manage without me?" she wailed.

"I'll manage for a while. You can begin breaking in a receptionist whenever you feel like it."

"But can we afford a salary?"

"Guess we'll have to, Honey. Guess I'll have to start asking more payment now as you've preached all along." His infectious grin brought a wan response from her.

"Run along." She waved him to the door. "I'll walk to the office shortly. Oh, Tom!" She threw her arms around his neck. "You really are happy, aren't you?"

"Really, truly happy, Honey!"

During the next three months, Kathryn located a retired nurse who was willing to help in the office as well as take care of the books. She found herself apologizing for the entries in the ledger under Accounts Received. To her amazement, Mrs. Inman's blue eyes twinkled.

"I understand all about that sort of thing, Mrs. Hammer. My father was a country doctor, and we girls used to help him with his books."

"You mean other doctors allow this haphazard type of payment?" Kathryn's voice registered disbelief.

Mrs. Inman nodded. "Especially in rural areas. Now don't worry about a thing. If I get stuck, I'll call."

But Kathryn had the feeling Mrs. Inman wouldn't have one bit of trouble. She radiated efficiency.

"One more thing, Mrs. Inman," she spoke firmly. "Always refer to my husband as Doctor, never *Doc.*"

Mrs. Inman soberly agreed.

*　　*　　*

Kathryn had come to this small community as a bride. She had never socialized much and had always worked in her husband's office. With no friends to keep her company, the succeeding months moved slowly. She discovered the enjoyment of cooking new dishes until Tom announced she must observe a strict diet. So she tried her hand at sewing—that was a ladylike occupation—thinking she could fashion maternity clothes. Her first attempt resulted in a tentlike effect that gave her the appearance of a tugboat. Tom refrained from a shout of hilarious laughter as she wept in frustration and self-pity.

"Look," he announced. "There's something you can do for me, now that you have the time."

"What?" she looked at him warily from swollen, red eyes.

"You know all the new medical information coming out in these pamphlets. I've often wished I had the time to clip some of those—you would know the important ones bearing on my particular work—and paste them in a classified scrapbook of sorts. You know what I mean? Do you think you'd mind doing that?"

She was ecstatic. "Mind? I'd love doing it! I've been so bored!"

"And forget about sewing. Guess I can collect enough to buy you what you need."

"How are the payments coming, Tom? I've deliberately not asked either you or Mrs. Inman."

"Fine, just fine."

"I don't believe you!"

"Are you calling me a liar, Mrs. Hammer? Me, the father of your child?" His eyes were mockingly tragic.

"Silly man!" But she let the subject drop and was content to have her mind occupied once more. Beside this new homework, she had the small rear bedroom repapered and furnished to receive the coming young one, now making his presence known. She found herself going more often to the small library to check out books. Then she discovered Miss Emily, whom she had thought was drab and colorless in her unvarying brown attire. Now she found the librarian was a fountain of knowledge, accompanied by a quiet humor. One day she impulsively invited her for dinner, and when the doctor came in, he heard the happy laughter and talk of the two women.

Good, he thought. She has always taken things too seriously and held herself aloof from these people.

Early one evening, toward the end of Kathryn's term, Dr. Hammer was called out to a poor, run-down farm. "Please let me go for the ride, Tom," she begged. "I'll just sit in the car and wait. I can't stand these walls anymore."

So she waited in the car, surveying the debris-filled yard, the sagging gate, the peeling paint. She shuddered as she thought, Another indigent family, so there'll be no pay. Why doesn't Doctor refer them to someone else?

Just then Tom came out, looking grave. "I'm going to have to take the boy to the hospital. I fear a ruptured appendix. They have no ice, but I used cold well water for a pack. Will you get in the backseat with him?"

"Of course." Her training asserted itself.

The seven-year-old was wrapped in a tattered quilt, and Tom laid him in the seat, his head in Kathryn's arms. The boy's dark eyes were large with pain and fear, mirroring the worry on his parents' faces. The thin, nervous woman was openly sniffling, while the gaunt, stooped man ran his fingers through straggly hair.

"Doc," he spoke. "Little Tad, he ain't a-gonna die, is he?"

"Milt, he *will* die if I don't get him to the hospital and operate. You folks follow me in your car."

"But Doc, how much does this 'ere operation cost?"

"Don't worry about that now, Milt. We'll work something out." Tom drove away, pushing the speed limit.

Kathryn, stroking the youngster's head, talked to him in a low monotone. "Just relax, Tad. Dr. Hammer is the *very best* doctor in the world, and he'll take care of you."

Tad spoke with effort. "Are you Miz Doc?"

"Yes, I am, Tad. Now I'm going to tell you a story about a horse, and you listen."

Tom silently blessed her way with the boy as he heard snatches of the story. And he thought of what a good mother she was going to be. As they pulled up to the emergency entrance, he noticed beads of perspiration on her face.

"Has this been too much strain for you?" he inquired anxiously as he gathered Tad in his arms.

"Oh no, Tom." She smiled brightly, awkwardly moving from the car to open the entrance door for him. She watched Tad being placed on a gurney and wheeled away, with her doctor barking orders. Suddenly a terrific contraction doubled her over, and she thought, This can't be happening. It isn't time!

28

As she straightened, the tense faces of Tad's parents swam into view.

"Oh, you're here." She spoke with effort. "You'd better go sit in the waiting room at the end of the corridor. The doctor will find you as soon as he's through."

"You all right, Miz Doc?" queried the man, Milt.

"Course she ain't, you big lummox," answered his wife with sudden spirit. "Here, Miz Doc, sit down." And to Milt, "You stay with her till I get back." A moment later she was back with a nurse.

*   *   *

Kathryn was unprepared for the spasms that took control of her body, as she obeyed orders to push. And all the bright lights. Why didn't they turn off some of those lights? And Tom. Why wasn't he here? And as they offered her a little gas, she gulped it. Her hands clenched the loops, and perspiration streamed from her head as she vowed she would *not* scream. When she thought there was no more strength left, she felt the body slip from hers and heard a strong, indignant cry . . . And there was Tom, bending over her hazy vision.

"Katy, my Love. Wake up and see your son! He's a redhead!"

There beside her was the naked, red-haired miracle. "He's beautiful, isn't he?" she asked weakly, not minding that Tom called her Katy.

"No boy wants to be called beautiful. But he's strong. I'm sorry I wasn't with you, Honey, but I hear you were a real trouper. I'm *so* proud of you, Katy, and thank you for your wonderful gift of a son." His eyes were brimming.

Katy put a hand in his. "I like my new name—it sounds very right. Little Tad—how is he?"

"He's going to be all right. Oh, Katy, my heart is so full. Now you rest and I'll be back." He leaned over and whispered, "Did I ever tell you that I love you?" Katy smiled happily.

*　　*　　*

During Kathryn's stay in the hospital, she was overcome by the many gestures of friendship from people who had previously been only names. Several women offered their services when she went home.

"We want to do something for Doc. He pulled my kid through pneumonia . . ." Or,

"I wouldn't be here today if it hadn't been for Doc . . ." Or,

"We ain't got much money, but I kin work real good and he'p you until you're on your feet . . ."

There were gifts for the baby, all speaking of the deep esteem in which these folk held their doc. All Katy's preconceived ideas as to what was fitting respect for her man's profession were forgotten. She glimpsed the heart of these people and their loyalty to Doc—a loyalty unfettered by monies. And now she was the recipient of some of their love and caring.

She asked Miss Emily, "Why is everyone so kind when they scarcely know me?"

"Honey, they've known Doc all his life, and they trust his judgment in picking a wife. They are extending their affection to you and the baby."

"But Miss Emily, I've been cold with them."

"You grew up in a different environment, and these folk knew that. They were giving you time to adjust. Now they are saying that you are one of us. Will you use these things Miss Murple knitted?"

"Our son will wear them on his very first outing! And do something for me, Miss Emily. In the lower drawer of the linen closet is a hand-crocheted table cover. Would you put it on the table and ask Miss Murple for a cup of tea? Tell her Mrs. Doc wants to thank her in person for her lovely gifts."

Tom, listening at the door, exclaimed to himself, "Katy, what a quick learner you are!"

Celebrating Life and Death

On April 11, 1982, at the close of our Easter service, our choir director announced that the choral benediction was to be the singing of Handel's "Hallelujah Chorus." He asked the congregation to join in. Having memorized it 50 years ago, it was easy for me to "join in."

It happened I was the only one in our section of the congregation who could sing the entire "Hallelujah." As we drove home, my husband said, "Don't ever again say that you are a has-been. Your voice soared on those high notes!"

"I don't know why my spirit felt so light," I answered. "That's why my voice soared—there was a wonderful lifting of my entire being!"

Soon after our return home, the phone rang. The minute my niece began speaking, I *knew* my sister Lois was gone. She said her mother died around 11:30 A.M., mountain standard time. As my husband and I traced the time, we knew why I sang the Handel chorus as I had: Lois's beautiful life was rising to meet her Lord, and my spirit had responded across the miles. We had been so close.

Lois was older than I, but we were as close as twins. Due to nerve loss resulting from the measles, she was hearing-impaired. She learned to lip-read by watching me and practicing it by looking in the mirror. I taught her to sing duets with me in her warm, rich alto voice. Lois and I shared dreams, giggles, and daring escapades as we grew up together. Gentle Lois, with the tender, brown eyes that sparkled and the big, hearty laugh that was twice her size!

Lois met the Master and dedicated her life to Him at an early age. After marrying a Wyoming rancher, she led him to a personal relationship with God. In July 1944, their only child was born, a beautiful red-haired girl. Six months later,

Glenn got Lois her first hearing aid, a bulky contraption that strapped to her thigh with wires that extended to her ears. When she wrote me that she had heard her baby's cry for the first time, it broke my heart. I hadn't realized how much she had suffered. By the time she died, the degeneration was almost total, but she and her husband held a prayer service each morning before beginning their chores. Pint-size, she carried large buckets of feed to the animals, cooked gargantuan meals for the shearers and other help, conducted a women's Bible study, and kept a neat house.

After Glenn's death in a plane crash, Lois brought her daughter to California to be near us. She suffered indignities and ridicule, yet she never complained or held resentment. When she was denied a rightful inheritance by greedy folk, she refused to take them to court, saying, "The Lord will care for me. Those people will answer to Him someday. I shall pray for them." And she forgave them.

She worked for Goodwill Industries for more than 15 years. People told me they often went into the store just for the joy of seeing Lois. She radiated joy and the love of God. Lois had faced reality and had achieved an abiding peace.

Her pastor read 1 Corinthians 13 at her memorial service, highlighting verses 4 to 12. He emphasized that her committed Christian life had touched and blessed many. Despite her handicap, she daily practiced the virtues Paul extolled. He finished by saying Lois was the most perfect Christian he had known.

The last two years of her life, Lois made her home with her daughter, Connie, and her family. Her loving influence wrapped all of them like a protective garment, especially her granddaughter, Crystal, who is deaf and partially blind due to rubella. The entire family learned sign language to communicate with Crystal, whose relationship with Mammaw Lois was unusually close.

After Lois's sudden death from a coronary, Crystal was

told that Mammaw had gone to live with God. The child wandered outside, searching the clouds above, feverishly "signing" to everyone. Where was her Mammaw?? Then Ben, Connie's husband, took Crystal into Lois's bedroom, opened her worn Bible, and explained that Crystal knew how this book was Mammaw's Map for living. God spoke to her through this Map, giving her right direction. Crystal folded her arms over her chest, and her young face lighted with an understanding smile.

Then Ben signed: "In Mammaw's Map, she read that if anyone was weary, she could find rest with God. Mammaw was very tired. God knew this and was ready to take her to live with Him. Now she is no longer tired. Mammaw is now one of God's special angels. Now we share her with God."

Crystal rocked with glee, her lovely face aglow. Sometime later, I passed the open door and saw her on her knees by the bed, Mammaw's open Bible before her. First she touched the Book as if her fingers were reading Braille, then lifted an illumined young face and signed heavenward. I didn't know if she was talking with her Heavenly Father or her beloved grandmother. I only know I was very moved by the picture. And I'm sure her pure-prayer effort reached a great and loving God.

There was weeping before the first Easter—then rejoicing when Christ's followers realized that His risen presence assured them of immortality. Last year we mourned Lois's death, knowing we grieved only for our own loss, for our Lois was joining in the heavenly Hallelujah Choir, her warm alto once more musically true.

Now, one year later, weeping has merged into a paean of praise for the life of one so finely attuned to the Infinite. This Easter we can celebrate Lois's and our own immortality as we affirm with Paul, "Death is swallowed up in victory" (1 Cor. 15:54).

Hallelujah!

Cry Not for Me

Cry not for me, nor pity show,
Else all my hard-won fortitude will vanish.
Daily must I be resolute, strong,
With vigorous spirit.

Should you desire to ease my task,
Just don't forget me!
Stop by occasionally
And be a sounding board.
Or phone me glad news.
Lighthearted, full of cheer.

Much strength is prayer-attained,
So pray that courage is my constant.
I've found our Lord does care!

But please—cry not for me, nor pity show,
Else I am stricken and defeated.

On Discarding an Old Friend

I was unaware of my deep affection
until the friend was gone . . .

There it stood in all its shabby dignity. The arms, extended in welcome, were tattered with tufts of cotton protruding here and there. The wide seat was distinguished by two sagging areas surrounded by the circle of lumps we had learned to avoid. The cover design was obliterated by the countless cleanings over the years except for the outside expanses, where English horsemen in all their gaudy trappings still rode to hounds, mounted on splendid steeds. The final deterioration, a split down the middle seam, had been decorously covered by an heirloom coverlet.

I eyed the couch speculatively, then said to my husband, "Let's get a new one. This one has had it!"

"Do you think so?" came his cautious reply. Typically male, he resents change. "Should we spend the money?"

"Look," I countered in a self-righteous tone. "You aren't home enough anymore to recognize how dilapidated some of our furniture is! This couch especially. Every time you order another book, you say, 'Man shall not live by bread alone.' Well, I think it time we indulged ourselves in a delectable dessert, in this case, a new couch!"

I hastened with, "I've never cashed those last two story checks, so we won't need to take too much from our expense account. See," whipping out a sheet of figures, "no need to charge a thing! No need to draw from our savings!" (My husband would wrap himself in a blanket, Indian style, before he would consent to buying anything on time, and our slowly accumulated savings account is as inviolate as the holy of holies!)

Now he threw up his hands in resignation. And, jubilantly, I went to the phone. The tired, worn couch was picked up by a Goodwill truck the next day, and soon after, a sleek, new replacement arrived. Some of the neighbors came in for coffee and to share in my bliss. They sat gingerly on the firm, plump cushions, remarked enthusiastically on the fine lines and color, then trooped to the kitchen, where they settled in the old kitchen chairs.

That evening my husband came in, sat first in one area, then another, then arose, saying, "Mighty fine couch. I'm glad you have it."

But he went to the bedroom and folded his length into the aged, creaking rocker.

My daughter brought in some of her teenage friends, who "Oohed" and "Ahed" how "neat" was the latest addition; but they, too, retired from its bright newness to drape themselves all over my girl's bedroom.

Well! Our living room had always been just that, *a living room!* Yet I found myself thinking that everyone now treated it like a showroom.

That night I was too excited to sleep. After the household quieted, I slipped out of bed and tiptoed to the living room. Turning on one lamp, I sat opposite the new couch, eyeing its gleaming presence. It looked as out of place as my face would with a small nose. It was a stranger in our home.

I remembered the sacrifices we had made in order to purchase the old couch. It was resplendent then, and gay. We had all been young together. It had received our two youngsters, never protesting their romping over its wide lap as they had grown. It had accompanied us as we moved across several states, taking a place of honor in one house after another. It had been sprawled over by young and old and had had numerous spills cleaned from its surface, and as it shared itself with us, had become dearer, more essential to us. It made into a bed and for years was our only spare; and now, as my nocturnal thoughts skipped through the past, a whole sea of faces marched before me as I recalled those who had slumbered in its depths.

I recalled how familiar and warm it had looked to us upon each return from a vacation, almost as if it spoke, "I've missed you. Welcome home!"

Another scene flashed to mind. My husband and I had spent an evening before the crackling fire, awaiting our son's return from a party held in a beautifully furnished home. When our 16-year-old came in, he flopped onto the faded couch while he relayed the high points of the evening. Then he paused, glanced around the room, and remarked for no apparent reason, "You know, I think we have the nicest home in town!" (Weary couch and all!)

Suddenly, my eyes misted as I remembered how the old couch had held a dear one as he breathed his last. How many times afterward I had smoothed my hand over its surface, seeking the feel of the departed presence! Yes, the old couch had been a faithful friend, sharing our hopes and sorrows. As the new furniture swam into focus, I realized it would be a long time before our hearts were wrapped around it.

It was with a sense of sadness, loss, and disloyalty that I turned off the lamp and crept back to bed. The children, now grown, would soon be leaving for their own lives, and this new furniture could never bring back the nostalgic memories of their childhood. Sentimentally, I decided that tomorrow I'd simply have to try and bring the old friend back home. Then I bolted upright as a glimmer of the future danced into mind. "But of course!" I exclaimed aloud.

"Uh-mm-mmm ... What's the matter?" groggily, from my mate's pillow.

"Oh, Honey," I chirruped gaily. "Can't you just see our grandchildren romping all over the new couch?"

Now it was his turn to sit up. He switched on the bed light and stared at me, horror-stricken.

"Have you lost your senses? Our kids aren't even married!"

"Of course they aren't. But they will be someday, and they will bring their children home to play on our new couch." My voice was dreamy.

In a "This must be the change of life" tone, he answered carefully, "Yes, Dear. All in due time. Shall we go to sleep now?"

Off went the light, and he burrowed under the covers. I composed myself for delayed slumber. My last happy thought was: The new couch will *become* a friend and will have its day, too!

About a Shy Little Boy

Judith Day was busy dusting her father's books when the doorbell interrupted her.

"Gwen," she called to her sister. "Can you get that? If it's Mrs. Jones wanting the missionary dues, they're in the cupboard on the second shelf." Judith heard the door open. Then . . .

"Judy," cried Gwen, rushing in. "It's a special delivery for you! Hurry and open it. Let's see who it's from!"

Judith looked at the postmark. "Why, it's from that little town I sang in last year. You know, I told you. Our college quartet sang at a funeral. I talked with their school superintendent." She ripped open the envelope and her voice shrilled.

"Oh, Gwen, the board wants me to come there and teach! A job, Gwen, a real job!"

Judith grabbed her sister around the waist, and the two of them waltzed over the floor.

"But Judy," panted Gwen, "did you want to go there? And how much will you get?" As she read the formal announcement, "$80.00 a month!" there was awe in her voice as she looked at her sister. Then very softly, "Why, Judy, you're crying."

"Oh, Gwen, I'm not really . . . only . . . now I can pay back my school debt and help Father and Mother a little. You can't know how I've yearned to do that and couldn't. And some new clothes. At last," she began gaily, "I'm on my way. Hot diggity!" and she whirled around the room.

"Girls, girls!" The authoritative voice of their mother sounded from the doorway. "What is going on here?" Her eyes swept the room. "And Judith, what have I told you about the use of slang? If you don't want to be a lady, try to remember that as a minister's daughter you must set an example."

Mrs. Day was a conscientious, sincere person, trying to conduct her living and that of her children with an eye open to "just what would the Pilgrims think." This time her rebuke was ignored by Judith, who interrupted.

"Mother, read this. I just got it." And she thrust the rumpled sheet under her mother's range of vision.

"Well, well, dear child, this may be just what you have been wanting. Have you told your father? Let's go and find him."

Thus it came about that Miss Judith Day took up her duties as first grade teacher in the mining town of Deauburg. It was with some misgiving that she looked into 40 upturned faces on her first day. Most of them were dirty and poorly clad. Most were Italian and Polish.

After a couple of weeks of school, she began to know each child personally. There was one youngster in particular, a tiny boy of five whose dark eyes followed her every move. His oval face lighted with pleasure when she paused at his desk to help him.

One day he shyly brought her a handful of wilted sunflowers. "Are these for me?" she smiled at him. He nodded, turned, and ran away.

Antone was bright, but he wasn't learning as fast as some of the slower children. This puzzled Judy. When she talked with him, he just sat and smiled. She made inquiries about the family and learned they were very poor.

"I don't care," she persisted to herself. "Antone is an exceptional child."

One night shortly after his sixth birthday, she called him to her after dismissing the others. "Antone," she said, "now that you are a whole year older, I've decided that I need you as my helper. I have lots of work to do, and I really need a little man about your size to help me sometimes. How would you like to be my special helper?"

His black eyes danced, but he answered rather skeptically. "How I a help-a you?"

"Well, I'll tell you. Every day I have to hang up coats and caps that have fallen to the floor. Now you could take care of that every morning and noon, don't you think?"

He nodded, dumb with delight. "And, of course, my very special helper always knows his lessons, now that he's all of six years."

Again he nodded, biting his lips in his excitement.

"All right, Antone, you may go now. Remember, I'm going to count on you."

He edged back to the door, smiling and nodding. Then just as he pushed the door closed, his husky little voice echoed, "Me help-a Mees-a Judy."

Judy purchased a large bottle of hand lotion. Each day, the children whose hands were clean were allowed to rub some of the "sweet stuff" on their hands. It was a ruse, to be sure, but she felt gratified over the results.

She kept a box of cleansing tissues handy for dirty little noses. The children were delighted with the soft, tinted wisps of paper—so much so that they began leaving their own handkerchiefs at home.

"Miss Judy," they would lie glibly, eyeing the drawer where the flimsy bits were kept, "I forgot my hankychief today."

Christmastime was drawing near. Each day the young voices of Room 1 practiced the carols and rehearsed the pageant Miss Judy had written for them.

As the evening for the program drew near, Judy had only one misgiving. Antone had missed school three days, and he had been given the part of Joseph. He knew his lines, and there was a striking appeal in his husky intonations, but he was needed for rehearsing.

42

On the evening of the fourth day of his absence, Judy walked through the little town till she saw a small hut surrounded by a few giant sycamores, bare and gaunt. As she approached, a yellow and white mongrel yelped a welcome and heralded her coming to the family. Almost rhythmically, the limp curtains were thrown aside, and curious faces flattened against the panes. But she didn't see Antone's.

A large man opened the door in response to her knock.

"Hello," she said, trying to sound very much at home. "I'm Antone's teacher, Miss Judy, and we've been missing him at school. Is he sick?"

"Awful nice you-a come heer-a, Mees. Antone, he gone to de-a countree; he help-a man."

"Help a man? Why, Antone's only a baby!" Miss Judy spoke before she considered her speech.

"Antone, he-a no babee, Mees. Heer," and he swept an arm around the room, "dees ees-a da bambino. Fine beeg gurl!" His tone was proud.

Miss Judy's eyes followed this motion, and she beheld a shapeless woman surrounded by children and holding a fat, dark-eyed baby. Quickly her eyes took in the sparsely furnished room.

"Oh, yes, the real baby. I see. But is Antone coming back? I need him at school to practice the Christmas program."

"Aw, he coming home-a tonight, Mees." The man's broad, white-toothed smile was very much like Antone's. Impulsively she thrust out her hand.

"Antone is a fine boy, and I'm glad to have met his father and mother. Tell him I'll be looking for him tomorrow."

The huge man nearly pumped her arm off, and both the man and woman nodded their heads in appreciation and smiled.

"Now I must go. Good-night. Here . . ." Again it was an

impulsive gesture. "Give this to the real baby." She put her blue, scented handkerchief in the man's hand.

The next morning Antone was waiting on the steps to greet her. To all of her questions as to his work, he would only grin, shake his head, and point to his feet. Puzzled, she watched him closely all day. But he seemed normal and very happy to be in school again. His lessons were improving, and her heart swelled with pride.

Almost before she realized it, the *night* arrived. She was costuming the little folks and warning them to speak plainly and sing very sweetly—"just like a violin."

"Yes, Antone, what do you want?"

He was tugging at her skirt. He grinned jubilantly and pointed to his feet. She saw a new pair of cow shoes—miles large for his feet. The entire situation dawned upon her: He had earned those shoes himself by staying away from his loved school for four days! Her eyes stung hotly as she smoothed back the black hair from the boy's eyes. Bless the dear baby—he really was only a baby!

Again he was tugging.

"Yes, Dear, they are simply lovely, and I'm very proud of you." Little Antone fairly glowed.

The three wise men had just beheld the star when someone in the audience yelled, "Hey! The curtain's a-fire!"

She looked. Dear God, yes! Right by the star! The audience had begun to cry out and mob up in an effort to get out of the building. Most of the children were backstage, whimpering and crying.

Oh, thought Judy, as she ran to the curtain, and tried beating out the flames with a book. I've got to stop this! It can't burn—*Dear God, don't let it burn!*

Her efforts were futile. Downstairs, the principal had succeeded in regaining partial order, and the people were being martialed out of the building.

"Children," she ordered, very sternly. "Take your places

44

in line. You will march out the back door and stay in line till I come to you. Marie, hush crying! Here . . ." as she threw wraps at them. "Put your coats around you and wait for Miss Judy. Now," as she tried to smile bravely, "forward, pass."

Somehow they stumbled out, and Judy gathered what remaining wraps she could find and followed them. They were surrounded by confusion, and she kept her group huddled around her.

Suddenly she cried out, "Where's Antone?"

He wasn't there. That meant he had to be in the building.

"Stay right here, children." Judy darted through the back door. The smoke was thick, and one side of the stage was blazing.

"Antone," she shrilled, "Antone . . . are you here? . . . Antone, where are you?" She raced backstage, coughing. At that moment she sighted him trying to beat out the flames with a book—just as he had seen her do. Swooping down upon him, she tore him away and carried him outside. His face was very white and hot; his eyes dark and luminous. She felt his hands and realized that they were blistered.

"Oh, Antone, Antone," she began to sob. "Whatever made you stay in there? Why didn't you march out with the others? Oh, your poor hands are so burned . . ."

Antone flashed a white smile at her, and his husky voice murmured happily, "Me-a help-a you-a."

The Other Side of the Coin

About 30 miles east of the sprawling city of Los Angeles, you will see a large sign on the freeway that proclaims:

"Welcome to Ladera Park
A Growing City of Happy People!"

Happy?

Now there is a word to ponder, and through the years I have done just that. Not that I am a philosopher, mind you: only a onetime horticulturist who has had time to think and reflect. My name, Prader, was once well-known to the successful citrus and avocado growers here on the West Coast, but that was a long time ago.

I find myself observing the frenetic strivings of those around me as they seek happiness. But I could tell them that their yardstick for measurement is all wrong. Happiness does not necessarily accompany living in an exclusive area surrounded by all the accoutrements of material success, yet this is what most people think.

As you continue on the freeway, you will come to an off-ramp marked "Melody Lane." Exiting here, you will soon find yourself winding through some of our California foothills from which sprouts silk-stocking suburbia. Your eyes roam over the carefully pedicured estates, and nestled in between are the subdued residences. They, too, are expensive, but not shouting the fact in vulgar display, and it was in one of these homes that the Mastersons lived.

David and Lita Masterson were numbered among Ladera's leading citizens. He was a highly successful real estate developer, and she was an interior decorator, equally prosperous. Their separate careers were complementary, as Lita always planned the furnishings of the model homes David exhibited. None of their fellow members of the Rolling Hills Country Club suspected that their public life was diametrically opposed to their private life—not even Celia, the maid—and the entire community was dazed with disbelief when they were killed.

As I told the police and the coroner, I heard the shots and found their bodies. I was their gardener. Celia swore under oath she had never heard one word of strife between them, always very polite, she said. When I was questioned, I pointed out that my work was outside, that my living quarters were far from the main house, so I had very little opportunity to observe how they got along, but that they always were polite. Mrs. Masterson was firm and exacting in what she wanted done around the place, and she was the one who gave the orders, but they were both considerate. All this I told the police, but I kept a few things to myself.

One morning I was trimming the privet hedge circling the drive. Mrs. Masterson had followed her husband outside, and I heard her say in a clipped voice, "Look, David, straighten your spine and be a man for a change! Business is business, and there's no room for sentiment where a commission is concerned. You sign up that Gorian tract today and quit waiting around for Fred So-and-so to raise his money!"

For only a moment, so fleeting I wasn't certain afterward my eyes registered correctly, a dark spasm of hatred crossed David's handsome features; then he quickly achieved composure and replied in a controlled monotone— and his words were unmistakable.

"Hard business. No sentiment. The warp and woof of your being. Doubtless you are right, but Lita," here his voice became pleading, "let me do things my way. I don't like the reputation you are building around me. I still think we have to consider *people* before—"

She interrupted imperiously. "But we *do* consider people, my dear. However else would we be where we are, had we not considered people?"

Then she laughed, her lovely face relieved from harshness, and she returned to the house.

"The Gorian tract, Darling, today."

That was all, but I realized there was an undercurrent of strife between them, that despite their wealth, position, and seeming harmony, they were unhappy. And I was saddened, remembering an early portion of my own marriage, long past, from which I had escaped by dwelling long years alone in Mexico.

As I said, I found their bodies. Celia was taking the afternoon and evening off, and I was working close to the house in case the Mastersons needed me. I spent that evening in my quarters, working on some of my wood carvings. Around nine o'clock I decided to take a stroll around the grounds before going to bed. As I put away the small figures and supplies in the drawers I had made for them, my eyes traveled up to the secret compartment I had fashioned under the eaves. No one would ever guess such a hiding place was there, and I knew how to shift the drawers to expose the tiny piano wire that opened it. For a moment I thought of the letter lying there, then I deliberately closed my mind to my unhappy past.

The night was cool and fragrant with the smell of newlycut grass and with star jasmine. I moved toward the virgin stand of gnarled California oak trees, reflecting that despite all disappointments, life was pleasant. And then I heard shouting coming from the house. I turned and quickened my pace. As I rounded the front of the L-shaped structure, I stepped into a stream of light pouring from the open door across the drive, and Mr. Masterson's voice, charged with fury, slapped me in the face.

"I tell you I'm *sick* of you and your perfect, pat answers!

48

I'm through dancing like a puppet at the end of your string! You've managed me for the last time, Lita. I told you that someday you'd push me too far; now you have! I'm leaving you, and you can pick up whatever pieces you please!"

Mrs. Masterson answered angrily, "You only think you're going to leave me! Remember, it was *my* money that set you up in business, and *my* contacts that have kept you going. Without me, people would discover you are nothing but a handsome hulk of namby-pamby brains! Despite all your talk, you like your public too well to leave them—and me—and we both know it!"

(Shades of the past, I thought, and shivered involuntarily as I maneuvered closer to the doorway.)

"Lita, I've been your rubber stamp too long. For a while I thought we could find happiness together—what a joke! I have nothing left for you, nor even any respect for myself! You've goaded me for the last time, do you hear?" His voice broke, hoarse with the long-pent, violent passion, and he suddenly whirled and snatched a gun from the desk drawer, aiming it with shaking hands as he continued.

"Never have you let me forget that I was weak! You are the brains, the powerhouse, and how you have enjoyed driving me! But no more, Lita! I'm through!"

"Put away that gun, you idiot," Mrs. Masterson replied, nonchalantly turning away from him to reach for a cigarette. "You haven't the guts to use a gun; remember how you acted on our one hunting trip? Quit being melodramatic. . . . Besides, you love me, don't you?" Her smile, as well as her voice, was mocking. "Here, give me a light."

The roar of the gun was her answer.

I tried to move my paralyzed limbs. I pushed up the steps, and my own voice cracked unnaturally as I entered the room.

"Mr. Masterson!"

He turned to regard me with dull, unseeing gaze, drained of all emotion. "I only meant to leave her, Prader, but she taunted me. She thought I loved her. I did once, but Prader, hate is the other side of the coin, and she flipped the coin. But I only meant to leave her."

"Here, Mr. Masterson." I began to edge into the lavishly furnished home. Already I could see a red stain spreading over the deep-piled carpet.

"Don't come any nearer, Prader!" David Masterson's gray face took on a little animation, and his eyes began to glitter.

"She was right, as always! I *am* weak. I never wanted all the things she did. All I ever asked for was a home and to be happy."

His last words hung between us like a child's plaintive cry as I read his face. I lunged toward him, but he was quicker, and he turned the weapon on himself. My momentum carried us both to the floor with a thud. As the air cleared, I saw he had aimed truly.

As I said at the inquest, I found their bodies and called the police. The coroner's verdict was that Mr. and Mrs. Masterson died at the hands of person or persons unknown, since no weapon could be found.

What I didn't tell them was that before I called the police, I took the gun and placed it in my secret compartment with the letter from the sister at the convent where Lita had grown up. The details of my past and the murder weapon will never be found because I tore away the tiny wire. Not even I can open the cache.

So why am I telling this now? Well, I am an old man now. Call it conscience, if you will, but I want to explain why I concealed the truth about Mr. and Mrs. Masterson. He was weak. I could sympathize with him, since I, too, had been considered weak. And he had wed a capable, ambitious, self-

50

ish woman who killed his spirit long before his gun snuffed out her life. I had once married such a ruthless person, but I escaped her. I had to give Mr. Masterson the dignity in death Lita denied him in life. I had to preserve his public image of a man with great strength, because I felt somewhat to blame for his unhappiness.

You see, I was Lita Masterson's father.

Mother and Son

Mayree eased off her shoes and dropped in the big arm-chair. She gazed at the litter of gay paper and ribbons scattered over the room. The celebration was over, the young people had departed for the club party, and Mayree was alone with the debris and thoughts.

"Oh, Rick," her heart cried out, "if only you were here! You would know what I should do!"

But her husband had died 18 months earlier, and this was her second Christmas without him. The first one had been permeated by his absence, but Mayree had been able to go through the traditional motions and events of the season because she knew this was what Rick would have wanted. And there had been her son, Gary, strong, comforting, steadying, so much like his father. This second Christmas without Rick found her trying to adjust to an encompassing loneliness she had never dreamed possible. For Mayree had lost Gary, too.

She tried to reconstruct what had transpired earlier, from the moment she had joyfully welcomed him home from the university. First she had dashed out through the drifting snowflakes when she saw his car nose into the drive. As he unfolded his lanky frame from behind the wheel, she had thrown her arms around him in greeting.

"Oh, Gary, it's *so* good to have you home again!"

Usually he picked her up in a bear hug, but this time he merely stood and suffered her warm expression. As she sensed his withdrawal, she stood back and her eyes searched his face. She only noticed a sad, unsure flicker in his gray eyes before he turned to help a girl from the car, and she heard his words, carefully spaced, as if rehearsed.

"Thank you, Mother. May I present Miss Carla Andrews, the girl I intend to marry? Carla, my mother, Mrs. Lovell."

Stiff, formal words from a stranger.

The girl was a surprise, too, although Mayree had known that someday Gary would take himself a wife. But she had expected him to let her know, to prepare her, not just suddenly conjure a pretty female out of the blue, one whose name he had never mentioned. Then, as she exchanged introductions with Carla, whose brown eyes were both direct and cold, she thought, Why, she dislikes me! And she doesn't even know me!

Then, This is why Gary was so aloof. He wasn't sure how I might react. Well, if this is the girl he has chosen, I'll love her until she'll just *have* to like me!

Then Mayree put an arm around Carla, exclaiming, "What a surprise! And the most perfect Christmas present you could bring me, Gary!"

As they stamped the snow from their feet and entered the house, she said, "I have always wished for a daughter, and now here you are. So very pretty, too!"

"Thank you," was Carla's polite reply.

"The guest room for Carla, Mother?" asked Gary.

"Yes, of course. And I'll get fresh towels and an extra cover for her bed." She scurried away as Gary carried the bags and led Carla down the hall.

The evening had been long and strained, with Mayree seeking to find the old rapport with her son and trying to establish a friendship with the young woman who was to become a part of her life. But she was rebuffed and held at arm's length.

After dinner the young couple listened to music from the hi-fi while Mayree washed the dishes alone. Several times unbidden tears dropped and mingled with the soapy dishwater. Once she found herself reflecting angrily, Why, they treat me as if I were another piece of furniture! And then her devotion to her son overwhelmed her, and she argued: He probably is not too sure of this important step he has taken. That must be why he seems so confused. And Carla is doubtless just as uncertain about her relationship with me. That's it! Well, I'll help them. Love is the greatest force in the world, and I'll just love Carla so much she'll *know* I have no reservations about her marrying my son. After all, Gary chose her just as Rick chose me. . . . I'll keep my arms and my heart wide open. Then Gary's confusion will lessen; I know it will!

With this settled in her mind, Mayree hummed along with the music drifting in from the other room as she finished putting away the last piece of china and hung the tea towels to dry. Then she went to her bedroom where Gary's wrapped Christmas gift dominated her corner desk. She thought fondly on this son of hers who would be entering medical school the following fall, and her heart swelled with pride in his desire to serve humanity. With light fingers she caressed the gaily tied microscope. She knew he would use it in the years ahead, and already shoved to the back of her thinking were the things she had done without as she saved toward his gift.

"He'll be pleased," she murmured, then began to wrap some remembrances for Carla. Mayree wasn't prepared with gifts for her, but she found an unopened bottle of cologne and a box of fine handkerchiefs, which she wrapped in bright paper. Then she remembered the glamorous nightgown packed away in tissue. It was one of Rick's last gifts to her, and she had never been able to bring herself to wear it. She only got it out occasionally to replenish the sachet enclosure and to weep a little in lonely remembrance. Now, the thought of the elegant nightwear kept recurring to her until she finally drew it from the drawer and spread it over her bed. She and the girl were near in size. It was really wrong to hoard such things when they could make others happy. It was wrong to hold on to her grief, too. And Rick would understand. Why, he'd be the first to urge her to give what was precious to her to the girl who was so very dear to their son.

Decided, her heart felt light as she wrapped this last gift for Carla. She joyously bore her offerings to the living room and placed them under the small tree and turned on the blue lights.

Blue is for loyalty, she thought, then went into the den, where Gary and Carla were now listening raptly to a recording of Beethoven's Fifth Symphony. She smiled, observing Carla's dark, curly head pillowed comfortably on her son's shoulder. She settled quietly in a chair to listen with them, studying meanwhile. She noted the girl's slim ankles, her fine structure, her generous mouth, and a strong chin.

She's a thoroughbred, with enough mind of her own. Gary chose well, I believe. Her sharing of his love for classical music seems genuine. They must have other compatible interests. They belong together just as Rick and I did. All this flashed through her mind as the pace of the orchestra accelerated into a torrential stream of symphonic sound.

When the concluding chord of the strings had ended, she heard herself saying brightly, "Well, you two look cozy, but if we are going to have our gift exchange before you leave for the party, we'd better get started. How about it, Gary?"

Gary glanced slowly at his watch as he arose from the couch.

"I suppose so," he answered without enthusiasm.

"Yes, General," Mayree thought she heard sotto voce from Carla; but no, surely she had misunderstood.

"I beg your pardon?" she asked.

"Nothing," Carla answered shortly.

Again Mayree felt a stab of pain, and she thought, Child, I'm not so hard to love or get along with. Ask Gary!

Ask any of his troop of friends he has brought home all his life!

But she only led the way to the living room, where the steady glow of the tree lights gave her sagging spirits a lift of courage.

They two had brought her a lovely brooch, which delighted her. Gary had remembered her preference for green, and the colored stones flashed a bit of white fire as she admired the pin on its bed of cotton.

Carla thanked her courteously for the cologne and the handkerchiefs, then started unwrapping the larger package. Mayree watched her closely as she shook out the chiffon loveliness.

"It's lovely, Mrs. Lovell! You shouldn't have!"

Mayree's eyes were moist, and she had to hold her arms tightly to her sides to still their trembling as she answered, "Much love to you, Carla, from me."

The girl looked directly into her eyes, and for one long moment Mayree sensed that with a bit more effort this young woman would be warm and responsive. Then the moment passed, and coldness returned to Carla's features.

Gary looked stunned as he tore the wraps from the microscope, and for a few minutes he was the excited boy of old as he examined and adjusted the instrument.

"Mom, this is the greatest! But how did you know? And the kind? And how could you afford it?"

Her heart sang as she recognized the artificial defenses were down, and he was once more Gary, not a stranger.

"Oh, I wrote Professor Talbot, and he advised me. Even ordered it for me!" She felt gay, almost dizzy. "Don't worry about affording it. I could!"

"Man, isn't this great, Carla? I'll be using this constantly in my research program at med school!"

"Great, Gary. Now thank your mother properly before we get ready for the party." Carla's cool, businesslike tone cut across Gary's exuberance like a knife, leaving his eyes confused and tormented again, while his face became the mask of a stranger.

"Yes. Well, thank you very much, Mother," he stated flatly.

Suddenly, Mayree could endure the situation no longer.

"Oh, Gary, what has happened to you? You aren't the same boy your dad and I reared! You treat me as if I were a stranger to you! I'm your mother!" The words were wrenched from her, and no longer did she try to hide her trembling or her deep hurt as she arose and faced Carla.

"Are you afraid he won't love you enough if he shows his mother affection? Have you poisoned his mind against me? If so, why? Aren't you mature enough to know that the heart has many rooms, and anyone like my son will love many people, many things? It's all a matter of degree."

She was pleading as she searched the girl's enormous dark eyes, aglitter now with unshed tears in a white face.

"Oh, my dear, I have known that someday he would find himself a wife. The love he feels for you is different than what he feels for me, but his love for you is stronger and more finer because of his affection for me. Can't you see that there is room for us both? And that the more one loves and gives of himself, the more capacity he develops for true, loyal affection?"

Her tears were falling from her face now, unheeded, unchecked. Carla stood and walked across the room to Gary, linking her arm through his.

"Mrs. Lovell, you are wrong. I don't resent you. I want us to be friends. But Gary and I are trying to help you." She turned to Gary. "Tell her, Gary. Tell her what Professor Talbot said. You owe her that!"

So Gary pushed Mayree gently back into the chair, beginning hesitantly, then suddenly his explanation came out with a rush. It was like a dam breaking, allowing the accumulated floodwaters to roll and tear furiously across the surrounding countryside. Stricken, Mayree listened as she heard herself labeled a "possessive" mother, one who desired to hold her son against his will and continue to direct his thinking.

"Ridiculous!" she managed to say.

"No, Mother, Professor Talbot says that unless I break the umbilical cord, as he puts it, that I will develop an Oedipus complex."

"A what?" she queried, so puzzled by all this talk that she really couldn't organize her thoughts.

Carla interrupted, "It's a term applied to a young man who develops too great a love for his mother, Mrs. Lovell. There is a legend—"

But now Mayree interrupted as she gripped the arms of her chair and sat up straight, cold wrath surging through her.

"Legend, myth, fairy tale! That's *just* what it is! And I'm sick of your wordy mouthings! Possessive indeed! Gary, you grew up engaging in sports, in scouting. You spent days at a time riding and fishing with your father. Your affection for him was as deep and natural for him as it was for me. I'm glad he didn't live to hear you soiling the very essence of what was always a fine family devotion. By accepting this . . . this tripe, you are repudiating your father as well as me. He was the most wonderful man you and I will ever know, and I had hoped that someday you would measure up to his stature. Now I'm not at all sure . . . I think you two had better go." Her voice rose as they continued to stand before her, perplexed, uncertain.

"Go, please! I want to be alone and think on this degrading idea your professor has instilled in your mind. My own education wasn't extensive enough, I can see, because along with the stretching of our gray matter was an emphasis upon character building and spiritual awareness. Your father and I believed that love, and healthy devotion to a cause or a person, is the greatest force for good in the world. To have someone who is trying theories on for size come along and undo what your father and I tried to build within you—well, that is too much! Go. I'll help you cut that imaginary umbilical cord!"

And she covered her face with her hands. Dimly she heard them moving in the other part of the house, and then she raised her eyes to Rick's picture on the mantel. His steadfast gaze almost mesmerized her as it seemed to her he was trying to speak. She heard Gary's "We're going now," but she didn't acknowledge him with either a glance or a reply. She heard the slam of the car doors, then the purr of the engine, then silence. Still she sat rooted in the chair, numbly trying to absorb all that the young people had said, searching the dear, familiar face on the mantel for support.

"Oedipus," she murmured. "I don't remember too well." She stirred, and found herself exhausted, but she forced her dragging steps into the den, where she located the term in the encyclopedia.

"How utterly awful!" she exclaimed. "Now how in the world could that professor make such a deduction when he only exchanged a couple of letters with me? He isn't a psychiatrist nor even a teacher of psychology. . . . Just *who* does he think he is to be dishing out such warped opinions to young people?"

She wandered back to the living room, eased off her shoes, and tried to marshal her thoughts. "Oh, Rick," she cried aloud. "If only you were here!"

But the house was silent. Even the clock striking the hour of eleven only accentuated the stillness and her loneliness. Never before had she felt so bereft, not even after Rick died, because then there had been Gary's strong arm to lean on. The thought crossed her mind that this, too, was death, different from the physical removal of a loved one but actually more poignant since it would be a living separation.

Habit forced her to gather the gift wraps from the floor, gradually bringing order to the cluttered room. As she performed the small tasks, Mayree found herself dwelling on the meaning of Christmas, the heralding of love and peace, and she felt a great barrenness within her. Her mind wandered to Gary's second celebration with them, when the tree lights and the carols had filled his small face with wonder. Then she remembered his third birthday cake, how he had plunged both hands into the icing, smearing it over his face and into his hair, while she and Rick had laughed until they were weak ... Then Gary's long illness when he was four, and she had nursed him day and night. The doctor had been cautious, promising nothing, only saying, "While there's life, there's hope." In desperation she had fallen on her knees, saying, "God, he's Your child. If he dies, give me courage. If he lives, I'll go on giving him back to You."

Mayree stopped smoothing the reusable paper and stared over at Rick's picture again. Almost it seemed there was a smile crinkling the corners of his eyes.

"Oh, my dear, I have my answer, haven't I? God knows my pain and sense of loss, but He also knows our son, so I'll put Gary into His care. Carla, too," she hastily amended. And suddenly the spirit of peace pervaded her being, and she knew that Christmas is not for one season but for always.

Turning off the tree lights, she went to her room and prepared for bed. The house was silent, but she no longer felt alone. There was a peace within that would sustain her through all accusations and misunderstandings, and some-day—someday she really would be able to help her children.

She was brushing her hair when she heard the click of the front door, then Gary's voice. "Mom, Mom, where are you?" There was a note of urgency in his repeated call. "Mom!"

"Oh, let them be safe," she prayed as she threw on a robe and sped to the living room where Gary and Carla stood, hand in hand, looking much like recalcitrant children. She sensed the dropping of their self-imposed barrier before they spoke, and they both spoke at once.

"Mom!"

She held her arms out wide and gathered them close! Carla was weeping softly.

"Oh, Mother Lovell, we were so wrong! Can you ever forgive us and learn to love me?"

"I don't have to learn to, Carla. I already do! And I'll love you more each year hereafter. Forgive? Of course I can forgive. That's part of loving you both!"

"Mom." Gary's deep voice was husky. "We never did go to the party. We went to Tony's and talked and realized that we had been a couple of gullible dupes! You see, we just got carried away by Talbot and his far-out ideas and let him influence us. Here I am admitting to you that I am in the wrong, and that's the very thing that got him started on your being 'possessive'! Silly, isn't it."

His eyes were pleading. "I've hurt you. It was so unnecessary. I'll make it up to you!"

Mayree's heart was bursting with the happiness that comes from being needed and loved.

"Of course it's silly, and I pity poor Professor Talbot now that my children have really come home. Merry Christmas, Dears! Carla, did I tell you that I have always wanted a daughter? I know it's late, but let's make some coffee and get acquainted!"

And they did, and love and peace blessed their Christmas Day.

End of Drought

Ah, the rains return, soft, gentle,
   persistent, and cleansing,
To our parched and thirsty earth.
And birds and flowers alike show welcome,
   while people—
Well, the tense lines on faces disappear
And give way to a softness, a wonder,
Almost a radiance.

And there are tears in my heart, soft, gentle,
   persistent, and cleansing,
Accompanying your return to my lonely spirit.
The ills, the hurts of yesterday are being erased,
And in their stead a rapture for life, for love,
   for you;
And on our faces a softness, a wonder,
Almost a radiance.

Tithing: A Continuing Pattern

This is the promise of blessing to the faithful: "Bring ye all the tithes into the storehouse, that there may be meat in mine house, and prove me now herewith, saith the Lord of hosts, if I will not open you the windows of heaven, and pour you out a blessing, that there shall not be room enough to receive it" (Mal. 3:10).

I grew up in a minister's household. Among my earliest recollections is the old red, Calumet baking powder tin, sporting the proud head of an Indian that served as our tithe can. Each offering my parents received was carefully counted, then 10 percent separated and placed in the Calumet can. We were taught that *that* top 10 percent didn't belong to us. It was the Lord's, and we were only the stewards or distributors of it. Thus we were indoctrinated.

The first year I taught school, my munificent salary was $65.00 per month, of which I set aside $6.50 as the Lord's. All my coworkers drew larger salaries than I, yet invariably they were out of money before the next paycheck and were borrowing from me. They'd say, "How can you afford to tithe on your small pay?" And I'd point out that my remaining 90 percent went further for me than their 100 percent for them.

Soon after Harold and I were married, we started our tithing program, and when our children began receiving allowances, they began the pattern, too. When they were in second and fifth grades, the church we were serving as music ministers launched into the building of an educational wing. My husband called a family council and spoke of how what we gave to that building would serve many people long after we were gone, but that we would need to sacrifice in order to contribute more than our regular giving. The children of-

63

fered to give half their allowances for a year, Father decided the 10-year-old car would hold together another year, while Mother tearfully whimpered, "I'll forget the carpeting for now." (Ten years of bare floors later, I got the carpeting!)

Well, that particular contribution resulted in an IRS investigation. Their query: *Why* would anyone, earning only a four-figure salary, give away a four-figure sum? Our photocopied checks, supported by church records, established we hadn't even reported all our "sharing." The outcome of that event was that the IRS got a lesson in tithing, and we received an unexpected refund, along with deep joy and satisfaction.

A few years later, our son was working for the Forest Service to augment our contributions to his college expenses. He sent all his checks to us for deposit. When he came down from the mountains to resume another college year, his account totaled a bit more than $800. His last Sunday at home, he placed a check for $100 in the St. Paul's offering. Later, I remarked that that was more than his tithe; his wide-grinned reply was, "A little extra was my thank-You for the times we were surrounded by flames, yet were able to escape."

Our daughter, too, continues this habit of money tithe as well as talent tithe. Her small church had no youth choir, so she has given her time and efforts toward establishing a high school and college-age choir, which has grown from a dozen to over two dozen beautiful young people. So tithing can become a continuing pattern from one generation to another. My mother used to say, "All you can hold in your poor, dead hands is what you have given away." So try this investment. You'll never lose! Besides, you'll just feel wonderful!

Dear Mr. President . . .

(For several days following the president's speech, Martha Smith had formed the letter in her mind. To ease her inner turmoil, she had finally put her thoughts on paper and in a sudden burst of courage had dashed to the corner mailbox and slipped the letter into the slot.)

The President of the United States
The White House
Washington, D.C.

Dear Mr. President:

We listened to your address the other night and commend you on your forthright approach to some grave problems. Your proposals gave every indication of having been weighed carefully. But I, the mother of a 20-year-old son, find my heart heavy as I recognize certain shades of preparation reminiscent of 20-odd years ago. At that time I bade my husband farewell at a small depot, while the "Hungry Five" played military marches, and everyone talked of "honor," "courage," and "right." My young husband assured me our separation would be short, "only for the duration, Honey!" I thought I knew what he meant, but I didn't. The "duration" has meant rearing his son alone with only a photograph, some combat ribbons, and the Navy Cross to make him real to his son.

What I wanted to write you was about our son. Dave is a fine, far-thinking boy. It was a great worry when he developed rheumatic fever before he was four years old, but with a move to a more temperate climate, care, and prayer, he has outgrown that disease. Participation in strenuous sports was denied him during his early years, and while abed those many months, his fingers developed a dexterity for carving and shaping beautiful objects. All these years his ambition was to be a pilot, "like my dad."

Our son is not lazy. Despite all the care lavished upon him, he was determined to overcome his illness and be independent. In high school, he learned photography and built his own darkroom; and when other 16-year-olds were unable to get jobs, he took pictures at clubs, weddings, camps, and churches. He earned his own enlarger, his clothes, and his "heap" of a runabout.

My son is generous and has a vast compassion for others. His first time at a church camp as a seventh grader, he placed his entire amount of spending money in the offering tray for needy children in an orphanage, happily forgoing the snacks between meals. While he was in junior high school, he gave me a milk-glass sugar and creamer for Mother's Day. One of his teachers later told me that Dave had saved his lunch money for weeks to buy this gift. During his last stay in the hospital, he was in a ward with an old man and a preschool child. The sister told me Dave would read to the little boy and help feed him, then take the old man's teeth, clean them for him, and straighten his covers. She said, "I didn't know that teenagers could be so thoughtful."

My son has courage, too, Mr. President. When the school bus skidded into the ditch and partially overturned, they told me Dave would have suffered no injuries except that he threw himself in front of a girl as a shield. His courage is more than physical as he stands up for whatever he feels is right for him. Like the time following a college play, someone decided to throw a "beer party." Dave doesn't choose to drink, so he suggested a "cola party" at his home for those who didn't drink. *Seventy* young people came to his party, overflowing the living room, kitchen, and patio!

Next year Dave will be a college senior. He earned part

of his school expense working summers for the Forest Service. He is tall, thin, with gray eyes, and muscles hard as steel. As his body has developed, so has his mind. I have always "preached" to him to have a reason for his belief and to be true to himself. Although I may not always agree with his thinking, I respect his searching for the "ultimate" in his own life.

His ambition now? He only wants to help humanity and is most interested in your Peace Program. He desires to build, not destroy. He yearns for mankind to employ love and tolerance rather than hate, greed, and force. Compassion, to him, is not a cliché, but the most potent force in the world, if mankind would spend money and effort exploring this resource instead of building weapons of destruction.

You are ordering more draftees to increase our military might. When my son is called, he will be castigated, reviled, possibly imprisoned, with the finger of shame pointed at him. "Coward," "Misfit," and "Lazy" are some of the epithets that will be hurled at him because he dares to stand by a principle. You see, sir, Dave is a conscientious objector.

His mother,
Martha Smith

A Weary Woman's Prayer

Be quiet, my soul, at this moment,
  Upreaching, receptive, and still.
Fine-tune every nerve of my being,
  Turn, turn my slow ear to His will.

Awash have I been in a sorrow,
  Continuous, heartbreakingly long.
My spirit, agonizing and broken,
  Seeks surcease, rest, comfort, and song.

Aching heart, accept promised peace,
  Pervading, far-reaching, and near;
Tired mind, cease striving for answers;
  Worn body, feel God's presence here.

Be quiet, my soul, at this moment,
  Upreaching, receptive, and still.
Fine-tune every nerve of my being,
  Turn, turn my slow ear to His will.

Too Many Gaps?

(A Commentary)

Sometime ago I ran across a friend I hadn't seen for months. I remembered her as vivacious, with sparkling wit and uninhibited laughter. Part of her charm was her display of perfect, white teeth. Now, as I greeted her, I missed that flashing smile. Her eyes still danced, and her warm personality reached out, but each time she laughed, up would go her hand to cover her mouth.

Sensing my observation, she proffered, "I know you are wondering why I hide my mouth. It's just that I am in the process of getting some bridgework done. Too many gaps! I feel self-conscious."

Then last Sunday, following our Gloria Patri, I glanced back over the congregation. Ours is a large, downtown church with a membership of over a thousand; the attendees Sunday were interspersed with many vacant spaces. I found myself thinking of the previous Sunday (Easter), when our edifice was packed for three services by folk decked out in gay, colorful finery. Our minister gave a powerful, thought-provoking message, based on 3 John 2:

"I wish above all things that thou mayest prosper and be in health, even as thy soul prospereth."

His comments were a challenge, and the crowds were attentive and receptive. But now, a week later, I wondered where all those people were. Too many gaps.

This week I have been mulling over these two episodes. In the first one, my friend was aware of the vacant spaces in her mouth and was determined to rectify the condition, not just for appearance' sake, but for aid in digestion, for *health.* And although she may suffer heart palpitation upon learning the cost of her dental work, this will not deter her. The bridgework has become a necessity in order to fill those unsightly gaps.

The absentees from church evidently feel no embarrassment in causing the noticeable spaces in the pews. "Let's go to the beach!" Or, "I'm tired from last night's party—too tired to get ready for church." If they should place themselves in the pulpit, visualizing all the empty spaces, how depressing it would be if *they* had to address a lot of wood. They might feel an inner urge, a real motivation to attend and fill those unsightly gaps.

Then with more serious consideration, they would realize that we all *need* this community worship for emotional and spiritual health and growth. As we mature, we are forced to admit to undeveloped gaps in our characters, our emotions, and our thinking. As we strive to fill those needs within us, we see the necessity of seeking and finding within our church home a *power* greater than our puny efforts to meet the vicissitudes of our lives, a *light* that will show us our needs (gaps), and then the necessary *bridgework* to fill those empty spaces. Somehow, as we strive for more perfect soul health, the cost becomes unimportant as we seek and find our great objective. The gaps in our lives are filled as we sense that His Word has become flesh and is dwelling within us.

Stolen Grapes

Dr. June, a psychologist, found a slow day drawing to a close. Just as she was about to leave the office and send Tami, her secretary, home, the buzzer sounded. Tami spoke on the interphone.

"A new patient here to see you. Shall I start the paperwork, or do you want to schedule her for another day?"

"Why don't you send her in for an acquaintance session? I'll take enough notes for your profile mock-up."

Dr. June greeted an attractive, 40-ish woman. Little by little she elicited from Dora Nestor her reason for seeking professional guidance. She established a first-name basis and then suggested Dora could just start telling her problem in her own way. "After all, I am here mostly to listen." She smiled.

"I can't forget the time I punished my son unjustly!" Dora's soft brown eyes glinted with tears.

"How old is your son now?"

"He's grown—almost through college."

"Does he hold this episode against you?"

"No . . . I doubt if he even remembers it. I'm the one who can't forget. The scene haunts me from time to time."

"Well." Dr. June took up a notebook, suggesting, "Why don't you just relate it to me in your own words? I may make notes, but I am listening."

Dora blew her nose and wiped her eyes, and Dr. June pushed the tissue box closer to her.

"Well, from the time our children were old enough to know the difference between right and wrong, my husband and I emphasized honesty, loyalty, and obedience. We were determined not to be overly permissive. After the children

71

reached school age, I made a rule that telling a lie would bring out the switch. Other misbehavior we would discuss and decide on what action to take.

"There was an early occurrence when Hal, only seven, returned from school with a new toy.

" 'Where did you get that?' I asked.

" 'From the dime store.'

" 'Where did you get the money to pay for it?'

" 'I didn't have any money, Mommy. I just took it.'

" 'But, Son, that's stealing! We never take what doesn't belong to us. Why would you do such a thing?'

" 'Some of the other kids did it.'

" 'No matter what the other kids do, you never, never steal. Now we are going to take that right back to the store, and you will return it to the manager and tell him what you did.' "

Dora's lips trembled a bit as she continued. "We went to the variety store, and I stood by as he confessed his guilt and returned the toy. His face was white, his eyes enormous, and I could see the wild pounding of his chest beneath his cowboy shirt. My heart ached. It would have been easier if I had talked with the manager and paid for the toy, but I felt Hal needed a lesson so that he'd never steal again. I was certain he had learned that lesson until months later when an agitated grandfather came to see me."

Dora blew her nose again and smiled timidly. "You probably won't think this important enough to keep me perturbed all these years."

Dr. June replied, "My dear lady, in my profession I refuse to consider any problem unimportant. A little burr under a horse's saddle can irritate him until he begins to buck! I sense you are at the bucking stage, so let's get that burr out in the open!"

Dora seemed more relaxed as she stood and turned to look out a window. "My youngsters were outside with neighbor children, playing. Grandpa, who lived next door, marched into the kitchen."

"'I've got to tell you something about young Hal,' he began. 'I saw him with the other children taking grapes from the Browns' vines. I called to them to stop, and when I talked to Hal about stealing those grapes, he denied it. Now it's bad enough to steal, but then to lie about it is a whole lot worse. I can't understand him. Believe me, his daddy never did anything like that!'

"As he relayed the incident, I felt sick with disappointment. His final declaration indicated that the waywardness of our son was a direct inheritance from me. I promised him I would take care of Hal. I called Hal in and confronted him with switch in hand, relating his grandfather's story. As I talked, I grew more distressed and my voice rose. 'And to think you didn't need the grapes. We have some in our own backyard. Then to deny stealing them when your own grandpa saw you. I shall never tolerate . . . *lying!* That is why I am switching you, and I hope you will never forget it!" Dora Nestor's voice broke, and she put a hand to her trembling mouth.

Dr. June interposed, "So, you did switch him?"

"Yes, and he promised never to do such a thing again. The next day, while Hal was in school, I saw Mrs. Brown in her backyard and called over to her that I was sorry my son had been one of the children to take grapes from her vines, but that I was sure he would never do such a thing again.

"'Oh, I told the group before I left for town to help themselves,' she answered. 'I had used all I wanted. They are most welcome to them.'"

Dora's voice lowered, softened. "Well, for a moment I thought I'd faint. I felt ill with regret, and I tried to will the hands of the clock to move faster. I was so anxious to see Hal come trudging up the walk. When I sighted him, his shirttail half out, dragging his sweater on the ground, my heart overflowed with love. I met him on the porch, dropped on my knees and held him close.

"'Darling,' I sobbed, 'can you ever forgive me? I punished you wrongly last night! Mrs. Brown told me today that she had told you children to help yourselves to her grapes. *Why* didn't you tell me that?'

"'Mommy,' he answered, 'I was too scared. And you never asked me.'"

Dora turned to face Dr. June, tears spilling down her cheeks. "You see, Doctor, I can never forget that my child was frightened of me. And I chastised him unjustly. I *hadn't* asked him. I had accepted someone else's report as gospel. I should have ... Oh, I go over and over what I *should* have done." She pulled out another tissue to mop her face.

Dr. June thought: My word, she has kept this in so long. Then she asked, "What did your husband say about the incident?"

Dora whispered, "I never had the courage to tell him."

"Well," asked Dr. June, "what was Hal's response to your apology?"

Dora smiled. "I begged him to forgive me and told him that being a parent didn't mean we didn't make mistakes. That last night I had made a bad one. That I had learned a needed lesson and would try to be a better mommy. And do you know what he answered? 'Aw, Mommy. A lot of times I've needed it when I didn't get it!'"

Dr. June put down her notebook and leaned forward. "Why, my dear lady," and she took Dora's hand in hers. "No wonder your son hasn't held this against you. He forgave you right then, when you asked, and then went on about the business of growing up and living. You didn't believe him enough to forgive yourself. You aren't the first parent to make a mistake, but you must have done some things very right, too. It seems to me you assumed this occurrence as your personal cross and have been doing penance all these years. You have built it all up into gargantuan importance. I'm sorry you have dissipated a lot of creative energy, grieving over something you could not bring yourself to forget. You are going to stop pulling it out, worrying it into a major event. And the quickest way is to start believing your son when he forgave you completely. Now we will work together to help you forgive yourself. After this cleansing experience, I predict it won't take long!"

When Dora Nestor left, she was wearing a serene expression, replacing the anxious one she had worn upon entering.

Planning an Evening Meal,
with Love

Tonight I'll create wondrous foods
For this loved family of mine.
Oh yes, I'll make the kind of pie
That Johnny likes: a quivering, choc'late
Mass, topped high with sweeted froth.

Jean's delicate, slender taste demands
A salad—crispy, curling.
I'll sprinkle cheese bits o'er the top,
And yes, a dash of something hot—
Perhaps paprika.

My lord is very stern. He wants his dish
Done—oh, just so!
I'll roll it oft in egg and crumbs,
Then brown it slowly, tenderly,
There in the oven. I know just how
His masculine taste will now respond!

Thus is my life composed,
Morning, noon, and night.
The same, same duties calling my attention.
The unsame dinners waiting preparation.
And yet, I like life so:
Old, constant tasks seeming new
To my shaping fingers.

Tramp Hound

Maggie set her shoulders in a straight, uncompromising line as she turned away from Chet's pleading. When she spoke, her voice was cold. "I will *not* have another dog around the place—especially a tramp hound! That's final, Chet!" And she picked up some breakfast dishes, carrying them to the sink.

Chet sighed, then answered softly, "All right, Maggie. I'll take him along to the gravel pit today and leave him someplace." He unfolded long legs from beneath the table and arose, pushing his chair back with a scraping sound.

"Here's your lunch." Maggie handed him the box while her large blue eyes looked beyond him over the vast, surrounding fields. Chet leaned over and kissed her gently on the cheek.

"Don't work too hard, Honey. It's going to be hot. I'll try to get home early this afternoon to unload the truck in the cool of the evening. 'Bye."

"G'bye, Chet." Her tone was lifeless, perfunctory, yet her eyes shifted to follow her husband's tall, lean figure onto the porch, where the object of their discussion arose and leaped joyfully toward the man who had shown him friendship. For a moment, Chet paused to ruffle the unkempt fur of the dog's neck, then said, "C'mon, Wag! You're goin' with me today."

Wag ran in circles of delight all the way to the shed where the truck was kept, barking continually. He sat proudly beside this new master as the truck left the yard and headed down the dusty lane.

The dusty road was one of the reasons for getting the gravel. The abandoned pit, 20 miles away, offered plenty of gravel to anyone who cared to dig and shovel. Chet had carted three loads during the summer. Their driveway was now in fine shape, as was the path to the barn. Chet hoped to gravel the lane to the highway before the fall rains commenced.

"I shore am tired having to leave the car parked at the highway jus' because of the mud," he spoke aloud. "Wonder if one big load would do it . . . Nope, think I'll get two." A whine answered him, and he glanced at the big dog perched beside him—a dog of no definite vintage. As they wheeled onto the highway and the truck picked up speed, he reached a hand over to stroke the hound's ears.

"Yep, you're several kinds, all right, but there's a strong shepherd or collie about your head. Me, I'm sort of chop suey myself. Pedigree never bothered me." He placed both hands on the steering wheel, and the dog shifted closer to him. "When I was a kid, my mother said, 'Every boy should have a dog, and every woman should have a daughter.' Well, she never did get her daughter until I married Maggie, but I had me a dog! Yes, sirree!" He was quiet for a while, then continued musing aloud.

"You see, Wag, that's the whole trouble. It isn't just you Maggie doesn't like; it's all your kind. I shore do hate to have to leave you someplace today, but I don't dare take you back with me. Tell you what, though, you may as well go to the pit with me and share my lunch. Would you like that, Boy?" At the rising inflection in the man's voice, Wag uttered a sharp bark, then cocked his head to one side, ears raised in attention. Both were lonely creatures, and each had responded to the other during the two days Wag had been at the ranch. . . .

Chet was taking the last bucket of warm, foamy milk to the separator house two evenings earlier when he spied the derelict dog sitting near the path. There was a shabby dignity about him.

"Well, hi, Stranger! Where'd you come from?" The dog shifted closer, yet kept a certain distance.

"You look powerful gaunt to me, Old Fella, as though you hadn't had a square meal for a while. How about some warm milk?" And Chet kicked over an old pan, filled it, then pushed it toward the animal. Slowly, the mongrel padded toward the outstretched offering, then lapped it hungrily. That was the beginning. The man made him a bed of gunnysacks in a lean-to near the shed, managed to smuggle out kitchen scraps, and found himself responding to the shaggy creature's affection. Chet called him Wag because of the constant motion of his shaggy tail. This morning, Wag had decided to come to the house to greet his master, which was the beginning of the end of his stay.

Chet glanced again at the dog beside him. "Don't blame her, Old Fella. Underneath it all, Maggie really has a soft heart. The doctor said to be patient and give her time, and that's what I'm trying to do. She had her own dog when we were married—a chow, he was, and that critter didn't like a soul except Maggie! He got mad when I'd even kiss Maggie g'bye! ... Got so she was trying to keep peace between me and Belden. Yep, that was his name. But the real trouble began after little Lissa was born. Belden was so jealous of our baby and all the attention we gave her that even Maggie said we'd have to get rid of him. We just didn't do it soon enough."

Wag whined soulfully, turned around once, then seated himself companionably closer to the man. He seemed to sense the undercurrent of grief in the man's voice.

"Maggie was real careful never to leave Lissa alone when Belden was in the house. That morning, she just put the baby down for her nap when the phone rang. Maggie is sure she closed the bedroom door ... mebbe it didn't latch ... First she heard a thud, then the baby screaming, and when she ran in, Belden was shaking Lissa like a rag doll."

79

Chet's voice stopped abruptly, and he ran a hand over his face. Wag crept even closer, resting a sympathetic head on the man's arm.

"Of course, Belden went, but our Lissa did too, and poor Maggie has sort of wrapped a shell around herself ever since." Chet looked down into the dog's compassionate brown eyes. "'Pears to me you understand everything I've said. Anyway, now you know why I can't take you back with me, but you shore have been a comfort to talk to. Well, here's our turn."

He left the highway to follow a narrow road that wound around and around, lower and lower, until they reached the floor of an excavated area. Then Chet backed the truck close to the hillside where he had been digging. As man and dog got down from the cab, Chet picked up a stick, threw it high, saying, "Go fetch it, Wag!"

With a shrill yip of glee, the dog bounded away, proudly returning with the stick in his mouth.

"Mebbe you are several varieties, Fella, but you shore are a smart one! Well, you go roaming as you please. I have an awful lot of work to do before that sun gets much higher."

Pulling on some work gloves, he lowered the tail section of the truck, got his scoop shovel, and began tossing gravel into the truck. At first, the dog stretched himself prone, head lowered to forepaws, eyes following the movement of the man as he methodically bent, scooped, lifted, tossed, bent, scooped, lifted, tossed. Then Wag stood and began sniffing around the area, occasionally turning toward Chet, who had dug out quite a hollow in the gravel.

"Go on, Wag," ordered Chet. "Go find yourself a rabbit to chase. I'll call you when it's time to eat."

He mopped the perspiration from his brow, then tied the red bandanna around his forehead. Without warning, an avalanche of rocks and sand, loosened by the burrowing, suddenly gave way and, with a quick, whooshing sound, buried the man and part of the truck. Chet only had time to throw an arm over his face, but that probably saved him from immediate smothering. As he lay on his back, he tried moving his feet; but as he did, the loose mass settled in closer to his body. Dimly, as if from a great distance, he could hear the excited barking of the dog, then the faint sound of scratching overhead. He knew the hound was trying to extricate him, but he could also feel the sand slipping and settling him into more of a vise. He realized his glasses had protected his eyes, and with his arm over his face he had secured a small air space. As he tried to take small sips of air, knowing the oxygen wouldn't last too long, he tried to think. Few people ever came to this abandoned pit. Maggie wouldn't worry until late afternoon—help could not possibly reach him before he suffocated. He recalled that different ones had told of how a panorama of their lives flashed before them as they faced death.

I must be an odd one, he thought. All I can think of is Maggie . . . her loneliness. She'll draw that shell closer around her after I'm gone. Poor Maggie, who used to be so full of life.

Suddenly he was aware he could no longer hear the faraway barking of the dog, nor any scratching at all, and the mound covering him seemed heavier. He found himself thinking his childhood prayer, "Now I lay me down to sleep," interspersed with "Hoped he'd dig . . . maybe just a small hole . . . to breathe . . . Poor Maggie . . . poor tramp hound."

Meanwhile, the dog had excitedly begun digging; but as fast as he made a dent in the loose shale, more would slide in. He whined piteously, then wheeled and started running over the surrounding ledges until he reached the rim of the basin. He didn't follow the winding road but veered straight for the highway, leaping over underbrush, tearing his way through brambles. When he reached the road, he stood barking at each approaching car. Some slowed, but all hastened on.

81

Wag finally sat on his haunches, lifted his nose heavenward, and began emitting a mournful howl as if he were sending forth his own canine petition. It was this pose that struck the fancy of Ben Goodlowe as he wheeled his pickup toward town. He slowed, amusement crinkling his tanned face as he heard the doleful sounds. Then as he came near, the dog began barking frantically, running down a rutty road a few paces, then dashing back to the pavement. Suddenly, Ben braked the car and put it in reverse.

"That dog's in trouble. He's trying to get attention."

As he pulled over to the side of the highway, he leaned out the window. "Hi, Fella. What's bothering you?"

Wag gave a series of staccato barks, wheeled to run down the old road, stopping to look back while barking frenziedly.

Ben removed his cap, scratched his head, saying to himself, "I do think that critter wants me to follow him, but nobody lives down that road. Nothing down that way but the old gravel pit. *Gravel pit!* That's it!" He gunned his motor and swung into the narrow tracks, bumping along after the swiftly racing dog. When he reached the rim overlooking the pit, he saw the half-buried truck. He descended as fast as he dared, but Wag cut straight down, and by the time Ben reached the embedded truck, the dog was scratching furiously at a mound of gravel.

"So that's it." Ben skidded to a stop and leaped from his pickup. "That truck looks sort of familiar. I've only got my snow shovel, but it'll have to do." And he began digging and scraping where the dog had, tossing the shale first one way, then the other. Then when Ben spied a bit of red bandanna, he worked faster, more carefully, while Wag circled and whined. Next Ben uncovered a man's denim-covered arm, which was crooked over his face. Hurriedly, he straightened the arm, feeling for the pulse. As he brushed more of the sand away, he exclaimed, "Why, it's Chet Masters!"

When he felt the faint flicker of response in the man's wrist, he let out a long sigh of relief, not realizing until then that he had been holding his own breath tensely. He began to hurry in extricating his neighbor. Wag began licking Chet's face, whining and pleading. Ben told him, "Just be patient, Fella. You go and sit!" Wag obeyed, but soon gave a high-pitched yelp. Ben turned to see Chet inhale a great gulp of air and slowly open his eyes. Ben leaned over him.

"Hi, Chet! Ben here. You just lie quiet a little longer until I finish uncovering you. Here, I'll dust off your glasses—shore lucky they didn't break. Now lie still. Don't want this stuff to shift again." And he continued to carefully scrape the gravel from Chet's body.

"Ya got quite a hound there . . . Stopped me on the highway. Purty near talked, he did, till I follered him down here. Didn't know you an' Maggie had 'nother dog—" He stopped, suddenly embarrassed, remembering their tragedy.

Chet, who had been slowly grasping what had transpired, found himself thinking of Maggie and knew that when she learned of the tramp hound's heroic performance, she would open her heart to having another dog. And he felt she would once more open her heart to life. His free hand reached for Wag, who slowly crept close to his master, whining softly.

"Yep, Ben. We got 'nother dog now. Name's Wag."

Remembering Jet

Last night I missed the little black dog,
  The little black dog named Jet,
The cocker with his floppy, black ears,
  The soulful eyes; I can't forget
His wet, inquisitive sniff in greeting
Us each time. He knew our meeting
Was always friendly. Before the fire
  He'd finally settle, at peace, content,
Except 'twas harder. The "boy" would tire
  More quickly these days. His years nigh spent,
His movements slow, his eyes were dim,
But because he was Jet, we all loved him.
Well, now he has gone, but we'll never forget
The little black cocker, the one called Jet.

Marriage Renewal

Sylvia stared out the window, unseeing, toward the rose garden. Again she was hearing hers and Jeff's angry voices raised at the breakfast table in heated argument. It seemed they argued at any provocation lately. What was becoming of their eight-year marriage? What had happened to the glow of oneness they had experienced during their first years together? Was there any purpose in continuing this unhappy relationship?

These questions reverberated through her mind as she thought of Jeff's last words. "The decision is up to you. I don't care!" With that he had stormed out of the house.

"Is it true?" she asked herself aloud, "that he really doesn't care?" Suddenly the tears coursed down her face, and she cried aloud. "But what shall I do? We can't go on this way. It's tearing us both to pieces!"

Suddenly she thought, The reason this is hurting us so much shows we *do* care! He *does* care! Her thoughts lingered over this idea awhile, then darted to decision. I'll go see Dr. Smith. I've known him since I was a little girl, and he married us. Maybe he can help us find a way out of our trouble.

Sylvia felt better just making this resolution as she hurriedly swept through the morning's tasks. Their home was a tastefully furnished ranch-style in one of the newer suburbs, an indication of Jeff's position as assistant to the president of a large plastics corporation. He had risen rapidly in the firm due to his creative initiative and ability to work with others. Jeff was tall with rugged features, steady gray eyes, and a quick smile. Sylvia was petite with black hair that contrasted with her violet eyes. Her skin was as translucent as Dresden china.

85

Their friends had regarded their marriage a model of perfection and were only recently aware of the undercurrent of hostility between them. There would be no words, yet the looks directed to each other spoke volumes. Their public facade was beginning to crack. Larry and Joy Hurst, their closest friends, had tried to penetrate the shell.

Joy finally confronted Sylvia one evening when they were alone. "What's eating you and Jeff?"

"Why nothing, Joy. Guess we're both tired tonight," Sylvia had answered with a set smile, then had changed the subject.

Larry, too, had been unsuccessful. "Listen, Jeff, we've known you two for a long time. Sylvia is one of the finest women in the world, and you—"

"Yes, isn't she?" Jeff interrupted. He, also, adroitly veered to another topic.

*   *   *

Sylvia sat in the outer office of Dr. Smith's study, impatiently tapping her foot. Her appointment had been set for eleven o'clock. Glancing obtrusively at her watch, she saw it was 10 minutes past the hour. Just then the buzzer sounded, and the secretary rose with a smile.

"Dr. Smith will see you now, Mrs. Carter."

As Sylvia went into the book-lined study, Dr. Smith came from around the desk to greet her, smiling his welcome as he took both her small hands in his.

"Well, well, Sylvia, my dear! It's always a pleasure to see you. The years don't change you. And how is your handsome husband? I haven't seen either of you for so long—to talk to, that is. . . . Here, take this chair."

Sylvia murmured that it *had* been awhile, really too long, since they had seen him to talk to, and Jeff was quite well.

"But Dr. Smith," she plunged in, "our marriage is simply falling apart! Jeff is pushing for a separation. I'm not sure I'm ready for that. I do know our lives can't go on much longer as they are."

"Whoa, Sylvia," he intervened. "You already have this separation pictured in your mind as a fait accompli! Begin at the beginning. What started all this disagreement?"

"Well," Sylvia brushed tears from her face. "You remember how ill I was for a while after we were married? I was in and out of the hospital, and our expenses were staggering. Jeff wasn't earning too much those days, yet he never complained about the medical bills or my inability to do anything around the house. We were so close in spirit then."

"Yes, I remember," commented Dr. Smith. "The doctors finally found what to do for your rare blood disease. You say Jeff never complained. I know that, but he was more worried than you realize. His devotion to you was exemplary."

"Well, that was true then. But where is his devotion now?" Sylvia burst out, while two spots of color stained her cheeks. "I have my health now. We have a lovely home and no financial worry. Yet he grows colder all the time. And we quarrel about nearly everything! Did his devotion fade as my health improved?"

"No, Sylvia. I don't think his devotion is any less, yet I think you have a point. I've known you since you were a child. During your illness, you turned to Jeff. You depended upon him for planning, for courage, for stability and security, and in that reliance on him, you made him feel very important and necessary to you. Do you follow me?"

"Yes, I guess I do." Doubtfully. "But I'm still dependent on him in many ways. Why would he want me ill again?"

"I didn't say he wished that, Sylvia. Far from it. Just think back over the past few years. As you grew stronger and more sure of yourself, how many times did you seek his opinion about anything? Like furnishing your new home, making social engagements, buying a new dress? Hmmh?"

"But he has told me many times that my taste is perfect, so why . . . ?" Sylvia's face registered confusion.

"Granted, my dear, Jeff would say that, since you do have good taste, and you represent near perfection in his eyes. But," and here the minister punctuated his words by stabbing the air with his forefinger, "Jeff is a man who needs to feel needed, who thrives on being consulted, not just by his company and friends, but by *you!*"

"Oh, Dr. Smith, I can't be the clinging type and just throw my own brains in the trash."

"No one's asking you to! But begin using those sharp brains by deferring to him in small ways. Try it, and you will help him feel he is a member of your team again. Another thing (and you can tell me to mind my own business): Don't you two want children?"

"That's another sore point, Dr. Smith." Sylvia brushed away quick tears. "We do want a family, but we haven't been successful. I suggested we adopt a baby, but Jeff just refuses."

"Maybe it's because the suggestion came from you . . . hmmh? Perhaps he resented your speaking of it before he had a chance to. . . . I'm saying maybe." The doctor's smile was rueful.

Sylvia's lower lip began to tremble as she accused, "You make me sound like a shrew! As if all that's gone wrong with our relationship has been my fault!"

"No, no, my dear." He leaned across the desk. "There are always two parties involved in any misunderstanding, and I'm certain he has faults that are galling to you. Mrs. Smith reminds me of mine every so often." At Sylvia's wisp of a smile, he continued.

"But if you can see one little way that you can cement the breaks that are separating you, shouldn't you give it a try? Give no more thought to who is at fault. Isn't this why you came to talk? You hoped I might help you find a way out of this trouble . . . hmmh?"

88

Sylvia stared at his homely, kind face for a long moment. "Oh, you're right, you're right. Strange I couldn't see this. Now you've given me something to work on, and I'll start right away!"

"Now," cautioned Dr. Smith, "you're all aglow with enthusiasm. Already you can see the end from the beginning, but remember: Your attitudes will not change overnight. Be patient with him if he doesn't respond immediately to your efforts. At least you are working toward a goal. Always do it in love, with patience, with prayer for guidance. And call me anytime you think you might need a shot in the arm!"

As Sylvia left the minister's office, she smiled at the secretary. Nothing has been changed, really, she mused. But I feel downright happy for the first time in a long time!

The phone was ringing shrilly as she entered the house. Running, she picked up the receiver and answered breathlessly. Jeff's voice was cool, accusing: "Sylvia, this is the second time I've tried to reach you. Where have you been?"

"Oh, I'm sorry. I was . . . outside." There, that really was the truth.

"Well, I called to say I won't be home for dinner. Board meeting. Maybe I'll just spend the night here."

"I understand. I'll miss you, Jeff." The last sentence was spoken softly, intimately.

"What? Oh, well, thanks." He sounded uncertain.

"Thank you, Jeff, for calling. I'll see you tomorrow evening then. That's Friday. Would you like any guests for dinner?" (I *will* defer to him!)

"Well, that's your department. Do what you want."

She persisted, "Whom would you like, if anyone?" (I'm still deferring to you, you lug!)

"Well, if you insist, we could have Joy and Larry over and go to the fight afterward. I have four tickets." She sensed his smile of wicked triumph, since he knew she de-

89

spised boxing matches, but she managed a "Fine. I'll call Joy right away, and see you tomorrow. Take care of yourself."

"Yes, of course. See you tomorrow." And she could tell he was puzzled as he said good-bye.

She laughed aloud and did a pirouette around the room before phoning Joy. "This is fun!"

*   *   *

For Friday's dinner, she prepared a light lemon cheesecake to follow his favorite chicken curry and rice dish. She dressed excitedly in a dress she knew Jeff liked. From the sanctuary of the glass curtains she saw his car pull into the drive. She squared her shoulders and walked out the door to greet him. He looked suspicious.

"Hey, what gives?"

"Nothing, Jeff. I'm glad you're home, that's all. Last night was lonely without you." She rubbed her cheek against the scratchy tweed of his coat. "How was the board meeting?"

"Well—oh, it was all right. The usual dull reports, with Chester whining a little because of the cut in his department."

"Oh, I didn't know about that," Sylvia told him as they entered the house together.

"No, I guess you didn't." He eyed her speculatively. Then, "Larry and Joy coming? Good. I'll take a quick shower and change. OK?"

"Whatever you like." She was demure.

He stared at her another minute before turning away. "This is a switch," she heard him mutter.

I guess it is, she thought. I guess it is.

That evening was the beginning of Sylvia's planned effort to revitalize her marriage. It wasn't easy to check the habit of quick judgment and unsolicited comments. Jeff remained suspicious and reserved. Some days, Sylvia felt frustrated and uncertain as to whether her new undertaking was having the desired effect. Then she phoned Dr. Smith for that "shot in the arm," and always his warm encouragement strengthened her resolve. One evening, Jeff actually forgot his reserve long enough to greet her with a bear hug, then held her at arm's length while he said, "You're a beautiful woman, Sylvia."

Once she would have replied, "You haven't told me that in a long time," but now she answered, "I have you to thank for that, Jeff. Any woman who has so much love and care from a good man is bound to be beautiful."

For a second, she thought that now they'd be able to communicate as in the early years; but the moment passed, and his face once more became inscrutable. Ah, this return to shared happiness was a slow, laborious process. Still there were times she wanted to beat her fists against his chest and wail, "Can't you see that I'm doing all I can to mend our broken fences? Can't you help me a little?"

One Sunday morning they listened to Dr. Smith speak about the meaning of Easter, of resurrection, of rebirth. On the way home, Sylvia's mind lingered on the sermon.

"Jeff," she spoke suddenly, "according to Dr. Smith, all things that die come to life again, in some form or another. Sometimes we don't appreciate the significance of portions of life until they are gone, but there is continual rebirth in and around us. Physical renewal, mental, emotional, as well as spiritual. . . . Do you believe that?"

"Well, yes, I believe I do." He allowed her the flicker of a glance. "But don't forget that the dying is sometimes a long and painful experience."

She knew then that he had caught her meaning and was saying in effect that his devotion had painfully withered. Was he suggesting that there wasn't enough life left in their relationship to germinate and flower again? Was he trying to

91

let her know that all her efforts to rekindle their flame of commitment had failed?

As they pulled into their drive, she asked softly, "But Jeff Darling, after such a death, wouldn't the resurrection be even more glorious?"

Then she was out of the car and into the house.

They ate their noon meal in silence. He wiped the cooking utensils afterward, as in the old days, but their movements were wooden, with no attempt at gaiety, each absorbed in separate thoughts. Sylvia answered the jangling phone with a heavy "Hello."

"Sylvia, my dear. Dr. Smith here. You know I haven't heard you and Jeff sing together for some time."

"We haven't, for some time," she replied quietly.

"Well, I have a big favor to ask and hope you and Jeff will give me an affirmative after talking it over. I've been asked to perform a simple wedding at the TB ward in our hospital. I so wish you and Jeff would add to the beauty of the service by singing. Would you, please, for an old man and a fine young couple?"

"Oh, we couldn't—" she began, then, "Well, you talk to Jeff. He's right here. Whatever he wants, we'll do."

"Good girl," she heard as she turned to hand the phone to Jeff. She heard his cautious answers, then he, too, said, "Well, whatever Sylvia says. Guess we could. . . . Sylvia?"

"Yes, Jeff. Guess we could." Her eyes shone.

Now they stood in this aseptic wing where white-gowned patients rested in white-draped beds. The young couple had determined that their wedding would not be postponed when tests revealed the groom had contracted tuberculosis. Everyone in the wedding party wore masks, tightened only at the top. Sylvia played the small electric organ that had been rolled in, and Jeff joined her in singing "Oh, Perfect Love," and "Through the Years," avoiding each other's eyes. Then the bride walked closer to where the groom lay. Her veil partially covered the mask she wore, and her eyes were alight with faith and devotion as the words of the old ceremony drew them together:

"Dearly Beloved, . . . wilt thou take this woman . . . for better, for worse, for richer, for poorer, in sickness and in health . . . ?"

Sylvia's hand reached for Jeff's, and his tightened over hers. They respoke their vows along with the young couple, but this time they were more than mere phrases. This time, as Dr. Smith intoned, "I now pronounce you man and wife," and the young bride threw a kiss to her new husband who, in turn, repeated the gesture, Sylvia and Jeff looked deeply into each other's eyes. It was a look that spoke of their agonies of misunderstandings, a look that beseeched forgiveness, a look that promised a glorious rebirth of their devotion.

*　　*　　*

Dr. Smith, observing, grinned slyly as he murmured to himself: "Another week, and then I'll tell them of that new baby up for adoption."

The Boy with the Lunch

Little did the freckle-faced youngster know that his open-hearted gesture would be the springboard to launch an ordinary reporter into an orbit of fame.

Twelve-year-old Mike Dunstan sat in the waiting room of the bus station in Los Angeles, watching the crowds of people. The loudspeaker blared forth from time to time:

"Your attention, please. Bus for Albuquerque now loading at gate four. Have your tickets ready." Or, "Bus from San Francisco now arriving at gate six. Departure time in 15 minutes."

Mike reached into his inside coat pocket to finger the ticket that insured his arriving home to Eugene, Oreg. He was returning in time to start school after spending a couple of months with his grandparents in Yucaipa. His parents had brought him in early summer, but now he was taking his first long solo trip, and he felt a little proud of his self-sufficiency. Grandma had given him instructions when they put him on the bus in Redlands for the two-hour ride to Los Angeles. "Keep your suitcase with you at all times. . . . Be sure to put your ticket back in this pocket after the driver tears off a part. . . . Check your billfold from time to time. . . . Don't trust strangers. . . . Telephone as soon as you get home. . . . And here is a lunch I've packed for you so that you won't need to buy much."

She thrust a large box into his arms.

Mike grinned. He knew the box held a mound of golden-fried chicken, thick slices of homemade bread spread generously with Grandma's own churned butter, and cake and cookies and fruit—more than he needed for the trip.

"Thanks a lot, Grammy," and he suffered a good-bye

94

kiss. Until this year he had sought the soft, warm fragrance of her arms, but now even his mother's kisses embarrassed him. He didn't know just why. Then he shook hands with Grandpa.

"Well, Mike," said Grandpa, "we look forward each year to your coming. Not as much excitement on the ranch as in town, hey?"

"It's different, Grandpa. But we had plenty of excitement when the forest fire got so close!" His blue eyes sparkled. Then he was on the bus, seated high above them. They suddenly looked small and stooped. There was a lump in his throat as he waved until they were out of sight.

All the way to Los Angeles, Mike recalled the special things he liked on the little ranch: the cow he learned to milk and the noisy turkeys Grandma raised. This was the first summer he hadn't run in fright from the big gobbler! The apple, cherry, and walnut trees. He had built a tree house in the walnut tree, often taking his meals up there to munch happily as his eyes roamed the surrounding hills.

After pulling into the Los Angeles station, Mike bought a postcard to send his grandparents. Then he settled down near his gate to watch the people.

"Excuse me, but could I use this seat?"

The woman's voice startled him as she indicated the place holding his large lunch carton. Mike glanced around and saw every seat was taken. "Sure," he replied, moving the box to the top of his suitcase in front of him.

"Thank you," she murmured, seating herself, then drew two small children to her lap.

Mike was young, but he noticed the worn-through sneakers on the children's feet, their faded, patched jeans. All three wore light sweaters that were frayed and shapeless. The children sat quietly while the young woman leaned back her head and closed her eyes.

Mike shifted his gaze from the woman's face to the big wall clock. Only eleven o'clock. His bus wouldn't leave for another hour, and he was hungry! He reached for the box Grammy had packed, untied the string, and lifted out a plump piece of chicken. As he bit into it, he happened to glance at the children next to him. Their eyes were large in their small faces, and they were staring, following each movement of the food to his mouth. Somehow, he knew these children were hungry. They were so thin. He thought of all the food in his box. Grandpa had warned him not to talk to strangers, but he couldn't have meant small kids! So Mike smiled at the older boy. "How'd you like a piece of chicken?"

The four-year-old nodded slowly, then as Mike handed him a drumstick, tore into it greedily. The younger boy began to whimper until Mike gave him some bread and butter. The lady opened her eyes, then sat up straight.

"Just a minute!" She spoke sternly. "Did they ask you for that?"

"No'm," Mike answered. "I wanted 'em to have some of the lunch my grammy packed for me. There's lots. See?" He held the box toward her. "Wouldn't you like some, too?"

The woman's eyes filled with sudden tears, and her lips began to quiver. "Sonny, I don't know who you are, but I sure do thank you for my kids."

"You take some, too!" urged Mike.

"We-ell, one piece, then . . . "

She, too, ate hungrily. Then she took a handkerchief, wiped her mouth, hands, and those of the boys.

"Listen, sonny, that's the first real food we've had in over a week. We had some crackers and a little canned milk. That chicken tasted like heaven!"

"Doesn't their daddy have a job?" queried Mike.

"He died, sonny, and I tried to work and take care of them until I got sick. The money went awful fast. I finally wrote my folks about everything, and they sent tickets to come on home, but we got two days on the bus, and all I could buy was some crackers. I hope you never know what it's like to get so hungry."

Mike's eyes were round with sympathy, then he shoved the box toward her. "Here, you and the kids take this. There's a lot left."

"Oh, no, we couldn't do that! Why, what would you do? Where are you going?"

Mike told her, then added, "But I've got a whole dollar, so I don't need all that food. Anyway," he said valiantly, "I'm sorta tired of fried chicken and Grammy's chocolate cake. Here, you take it!"

The loudspeaker blared, "Bus for Kansas City now loading at gate two. Have your tickets ready."

"Oh, that's our bus!" exclaimed the lady. "Thanks again. You'll never know . . ." And she began gathering her few dilapidated pieces of luggage together, giving the four-year-old a small case to carry. Mike quickly tied the lunch box securely and followed them to their line.

"Here, lady, I meant it. I want you to take this along for your kids."

Her mouth began to tremble again, and Mike's freckled face flushed with embarrassment.

"Thanks," she whispered. She smiled, and her defeat and weariness seemed to evaporate as her shoulders straightened with a gesture of restored courage.

*   *   *

Ted Rafferty was a reporter for the *Daily Ledger.* He was tired. Not so tired in body but weary of the mundane assignments that had fallen to him. Resentment smoldered within him. Not once had he gotten a scoop on anything worthwhile to which he could proudly attach his byline. Well, his vacation commenced the next day, and was he ever ready for it!

He'd loaf and fish and forget about the feverish world of copy, editing, deadlines. Yes, sirree! He would get that constant smell of printer's ink out of his nostrils. He wouldn't even look at anything that resembled print. At this moment, however, he hunched over his desk, completing some final rewrite of a perfunctory report on a pallid subject. The copy-boy breezed by, saying, "Boss wants to see you."

Ted stopped typing to stare after the scurrying boy. "Sure, just drop everything and run!"

He deliberately finished typing the page before going to the editor's office.

"You wished to see me, sir?" he asked respectfully.

"Yes. Sit down, Ted." Mr. Cartwright motioned to a chair. "Understand you go on vacation tomorrow. Want to say a few things so that you can be thinking about them."

He paused to study the tall young man whose face mirrored his dissatisfaction, then proceeded quietly. "When you started with us a year ago, I was certain you had the makings of a top reporter. Seldom have I been wrong in my hunches, but lately I've been questioning my early appraisal of you."

Ted sat quietly, but inside he was tensing like a coiled spring as he wondered whether this was a preamble to firing him. The chief's voice had a raspy quality. His shrewd, brown eyes were direct.

"Ted, some of your reports have been written with a flourish, but most of them haven't. I've waited for you to catch fire, but you grind out the same trite stuff. Look, I want you to dig for the story *behind* the story. Do you follow me? Give me some *heart* in your accounts of people and events."

"Well, sir," Ted's voice was unenthusiastic, "my assignments have been just that—dull—as you must have known. Not much opportunity to do more than relate facts, but isn't that what every good reporter does?"

"Nonsense! Are you going to be satisfied with merely

98

being good, or do you want to be great? You have the ability to become more than good. Sure, get the facts and get them straight, but don't stop with that. Try digging below the surface as to what prompted this or that. Look under a few rocks. Study people, question them, find out what makes them tick, and report your facts against that human background. Then your reporting will never be dull or routine. Your stories will breathe!" He stopped as he saw a flicker of response in Ted's eyes.

The boss held out his hand as they both stood. "Well, that's what I wanted to say. Where are you going?"

Ted told him.

"Have a good time then. If you run across a good story, fire it to me. That's all."

The next morning found Ted sitting in the bus station, waiting for the coach that would take him to that jeweled lake in northern California. There he would put out of his mind the words of the chief, words that had stung his pride.

Sitting on one side of a young lad, he found himself observing the episode of the lunch. Suddenly, he knew this was a made-to-order human interest story. His excitement grew, and he thought that this was what the boss meant about catching fire.

When Mike resumed his seat after giving the little family his carton of food, Ted spoke to him. "That was a mighty fine thing you just did, son."

Mike's face crimsoned again, and he rubbed one foot over the other.

"Listen, kid, I work for a newspaper, and my name is Ted. I'm on a vacation, and I heard you tell that lady you were going to Oregon. Well, I'll be going your way for some time, and you're the kind of seatmate I'd like. How about it? What's your name?"

"Mike, sir. I never knew a newspaperman before. Sure, I guess you can sit with me."

All afternoon Mike chattered about his home, his summer, his dog, until he fell asleep propped against the rough tweed of Ted's jacket. Ted was forming the story in his mind with something teasing him about the situation—a parallel. Had someone else already written his story? And then, just as they neared Eureka, where he was getting off, he knew what was nagging him.

He told Mike good-bye, slipped another dollar into his pocket, and hurried to a small hotel. He would rent a typewriter and get his story to the chief. He grinned, picturing the boss's surprise upon getting something from him so soon. He could feel this story growing within him, a sensation he had never known before. When he was shown his room, he picked up the Gideon Bible before even loosening his tie, and began leafing and searching. An hour later a slow smile creased his face as he found in John 6 what had been teasing him.

"There is a lad here, which hath five barley loaves, and two small fishes" (v. 9). The miracle of feeding the 5,000 followed.

Ted rang for paper, lots of it, and a typewriter. He rolled up his sleeves and began pounding out his story, one that was to be reprinted across the country, presented in capsule form to television viewers, and destined to make his byline as familiar as a newspaper itself. He wrote of a modern-day miracle he had observed, the miracle of compassion, of sharing, of renewed hope and courage. And his characters lived and breathed, so that his editor was filled with excitement even as his eyes filled with tears. Ted's title: "There Was a Boy with a Lunch."

*Life, as well as death, lay in her hands, but
Lt. Virginia Cogswell flew to meet*

Moments of Decision

Virginia Cogswell awakened even before the shrill ringing of the telephone sliced through the early morning stillness. She answered in a sleep-drugged voice. "Lieutenant Cogswell here."

The unhurried, smooth, male voice roused her with its cheerful impersonality. "Lieutenant, Flight 205 has been scheduled to depart here in another hour with 30 patients aboard. How soon can you be ready for a pickup?"

"Very soon. I'll breakfast at MATS* operation before I load the patients."

"Right," he responded, and the line clicked dead.

For one luxurious moment, Virginia lingered in the warm bed. She had flown into Travis 24 hours earlier, had seen her patients safely into waiting ambulances, made her report, then used free time to do laundry and catch up on mail before hitting the sack, bone weary. Well, this was her life, and she had much to do during the next hour. She donned her flight suit in 10 minutes.

It was 4 A.M., a crisp morning and still dark. First Lt. Virginia Cogswell was a flight nurse assigned to Air Evac** for a period of 18 months. She was tall, slim, with beautiful gray eyes and brown hair just touched with gray at the temples. She wasn't quite 30.

En route to the PMC*** office, she stopped at the Mil-

*Military Airport Transport Service.
**Air Evacuation.
***Patient Movement Control.

itary Airport Transport Service to pick up the manifest
charts of her patients. It was then she learned that this
flight was to be her complete responsibility—her first run
alone. Her flight school training and the half-dozen evacu-
ations she had accompanied as an assistant were now going
to be put to the test. Her hands trembled as she picked up
the list of patients' names, checking their ailments carefully.
She noted the type of medication and special care that
would be required, then proceeded to order the necessary
supplies. Her eyes ran down the list of litter patients: there
were leukemia, concussion, some leg fractures, a cardiac.

She thought to herself, Pretty much run-of-the-mill.
We get a little of everything, so I'll need a little of everything.
Must be sure to have plenty of oxygen. It could be rough.

She scrutinized her manifest charts. She was to be
solely responsible for the well-being of 30 ill people while
they were airborne, and should she be remiss in having the
right drugs aboard, or not enough provisions, it would go on
her record in Washington. Virginia was very conscientious,
regarding her work with dedication. That quality of giving of
herself may have been one of the reasons she had been called
upon when the Air Evac had carried more seriously ill or
injured persons.

Leaving the hospital, she directed the driver to take her
to the flight line so that she could check the plane's interior.
The pilot and copilot greeted her.

"Come on, Angel," they urged her. "Everything's ship-
shape. We just have time for a bit of chow."

"I'll join you in a minute. I must be sure about the space
aboard. One diabetic, and one ulcer . . . " This last was spoken more to herself, although she smiled at them.

"Aw, you're too particular," they teased as they left the
plane and sauntered toward the lunchroom, but they were
pleased to be flying this quietly efficient nurse. In a few

minutes she slipped onto a stool beside them at the counter. They had already placed her order for one crisp waffle, two strips of bacon, and a mug of black coffee.

"Captain Porter, you and Captain James are the greatest!" Virginia sighed gratefully.

"Thank you, ma'am," Copilot James answered soberly. "We just can't help ourselves!"

By the time they had finished breakfast, it was time for her to return to the hospital to accompany the patients in the ambulance-bus to the plane. She directed the placing of each one, thinking of his comfort as well as ease of service. Then it was time to check the food and medical supplies into the airship with two medical technicians to assist her. Some of her charges would be taken short distances to other hospitals, but termination of this flight was to be at McCord Air Force Base after zigzagging cross-country. There would also be a return load of ambulatory or bed patients to be shifted to various hospitals.

Just as she remarked, "Well, that's everything," a car swept up with screeching brakes. Up the ramp puffed a very pregnant woman followed by the taxi driver carrying her luggage.

"Oh, Lieutenant," chirruped the woman sweetly. "I understand this flight will be stopping at Andrews Air Force Base, and that is my destination. I decided I had to go there to have my baby—near my husband, you know," she finished archly.

Lieutenant Cogswell glanced at her manifest of patients. "What is your name, please?"

"I am Mrs. Anthony von Tilden, but you won't find my name there. All I want is a ride."

"Mrs. von Tilden, may I ask how close is your delivery date?" Virginia guessed that she was well into her ninth month.

"Well, *really!* I think it's most impertinent of you to ask that, but I'll tell you that the baby isn't due for another two or three weeks, so you won't have a thing to worry about!" Then her tone softened and became wheedling. "All I need is a little old seat."

"Mrs. von Tilden, I only follow orders, and we are not allowed to take any women on these flights who are past eight months in pregnancy. We aren't equipped for complications that might occur during delivery. With all my other patients, I couldn't possibly handle their needs, plus yours, should you go into labor. I'm sorry, but I'm afraid you can't take this plane." Virginia's voice was firm.

"Young lady, I'll have you know that my husband is a lieutenant colonel, and he knows *all* the brass back in Washington! He can have you demoted for this . . . this insufferable conduct!" Mrs. von Tilden's strident tones were carrying into the plane; then she became charming once more.

"Oh, honey, you won't even hear a peep out of me. But I simply have to go!"

Lieutenant Cogswell tried to placate her while getting her away from the plane. "Now, Mrs. von Tilden, you've been around the service long enough to know that I am only doing my duty and following orders. Let's go over to the PMC office. They'd have to clear you anyway."

When she explained the situation to the officer in charge and mentioned the name von Tilden, he shifted uneasily and finally said, "Well, we *do* have such orders. However, I'll leave the final decision to Lieutenant Cogswell, as this flight is entirely in her charge."

"No help here," breathed Virginia to herself. She turned and carefully appraised the irate mother-to-be, then declared, "I'm sorry, but I feel you'd be risking your life and that of your baby if you took this flight. It's obvious that you are due anytime. With the load of patients we now have, I simply couldn't care for them adequately if you were with us and went into labor. Now I must go. We are ready for take-off. Really, I'm sorry." She tried to smile at her new adversary, but her face felt stiff, and her heart was heavy. There was a slight possibility she could be demoted for this action, but in good conscience she felt her decision must stand.

Long after being airborne, despite her activity in the easing of tractions, the loosening or tightening of bandages, and the myriad other chores in ministering to her air patients, her mind kept harking back to the unpleasant incident and the possible unpleasant aftermath. She sighed inwardly, trying to put it from her mind.

They were flying over the Midwest when her cardiac case began having difficulty. She gave him a shot of morphine, then called over the intercom to Captain Porter.

"Could we fly at a lower altitude, Captain? One of my men is having difficulty. Lower elevation might help."

"Will do," sang his warm reply. He was so near, yet seemed so far away. Everyone was far away from her as the big ship plowed through the skies. Her world was this confined space, hung with litters carrying maimed and ill bodies that were entrusted to her for several long hours. The plane went to the lower altitude, but her heart patient was not eased.

"Captain, what place are we near?"

"One minute, Lieutenant." After a pause, he continued. "In Kansas between a little place called Montezuma and Dodge City."

"Please radio Dodge. Ask if a military plane can land there. If possible, we must land. My patient's response to his morphine shot is poor. He needs a hospital. Ask for a doctor and ambulance to meet us. Explain his heart condition. I have him on oxygen."

"Will do, Lieutenant," the captain responded in a sure

voice. The remainder of her charges received only cursory attention during the next few minutes, and she was relieved when the captain announced: "We are landing at Dodge in two minutes. Doctor and ambulance standing by."

As she removed the oxygen mask from the man's face and wiped the perspiration from his brow, she said gently, "Just relax. You're going to be all right. A doctor and ambulance are waiting to take you to a hospital, and you can be picked up on another trip."

His pain-drenched eyes were grateful. Suddenly they were wheeling him off the plane. He managed a wan, sweet smile for her, and her spirits were lifted.

Shortly after they were airborne again, they encountered lightning and driving sheets of rain, which caused uneasiness among her patients. Soon the air turbulence became so violent that the pilot called to say that he was going to try and get above the storm. "But keep me informed about your charges," he added.

The group on the plane began to settle down once more as she checked on each one's comfort. It was time for this one's injection, and that one's bandages must be changed, and her ulcer patient was ready for a small cup of creamy milk. As she tended one person, her ready smile would flash to the next one, and a sort of camaraderie hovered between them. She was swinging into the stride of routine care when she heard a gasping call from the forward part of the ship. Hurrying, she reached the man who was choking and gasping for breath. She saw that his throat had become so swollen that it was obstructing the air passage. It was clear that a tracheotomy was needed, but could *she* do it? She had observed and assisted doctors with this minor operation a number of times, but to perform it alone! Could she? While these thoughts were flashing through her mind, she was automatically getting her kit of sterile instruments, which were always kept ready for an emergency. There was no other course open to her, and no one she could turn to or depend on; and this man's life depended on her skill!

"God," she breathed, "help me now."

She talked soothingly to him. "Just relax now ... I'm going to help you breathe, but you mustn't fight me ... Just relax now ... It will only hurt for a minute ..."

While she was sterilizing the throat area, she was remembering that the trachea was only about four inches long and three-quarters of an inch in diameter and just below the larynx. The scalpel must be applied ... just ... about *here,* and she made the small incision, quickly and deftly, followed by the rapid insertion of the curved metal tube. Even before she had applied the small sterile bandage to the wound, she could see his whole body relax and his color return to normal. Suddenly she felt faint and light-headed. Then she recalled that she had fed the others but had only taken time for a cup of coffee for herself. And that 4:35 breakfast seemed like a thousand years ago!

She weaved her way to the food compartment and opened a box lunch. Sitting down, she munched a cold ham sandwich, and despite her weariness, she found herself thinking a short prayer. *Thank You, God. ... Ah, I'm so happy You helped me do it.*

"Lieutenant," came Captain Porter's voice. "Are you with us? How are all the children?"

"All here, thank you, Captain. I was just going to ask you to go down again to a lower altitude."

"Will do. ... Oh, we thought you'd be interested in a radio message we just received. There's a new von Tilden heir back at Travis—"

"No!" she exclaimed. Then, "Well, I'm glad it happened there instead of here! Listen, radio ahead to Fort Leavenworth and have a doctor in one of the ambulances, with

107

oxygen. I had to do a quick tracheotomy, and the man needs hospitalization."

Copilot James exploded. "Hey there! What are you, anyway!"

"Only a flight nurse, Captain. It's all in a day's work."

The Second Mile*

I was nearing the end of my first year of teaching in a small, consolidated Illinois school. My salary of $65.00 a month had been stretched to cover room, board, clothes, and incidentals in the depression-ridden year of 1937. I had managed to pay off one of my college loans and had enough left to buy a bus ticket to a vacation job in Wyoming.

Experienced as I was at cutting economic corners, I had done very little traveling alone. I packed my warm, heavy clothes and left them with my Illinois landlady until my return in September. For my trip I wore a summer knit suit, "so I won't look too wrinkled when I get there!" But I had not anticipated the frigid mountain air at night. The slight cold I had developed near the end of school intensified during the trip, so that by the time we were approaching Cheyenne, my constant cough was disturbing everyone.

There were a number of transfers involved en route; and as I boarded each new bus, I breathed a sigh of relief to find the first seat behind the driver vacant. Sitting near the driver gave me a sense of safety.

It was after 9 P.M. when we pulled out of Cheyenne, and soon the flow of conversation dwindled to a trickle as travelers settled down to sleep. I curled up in my seat, hugging my lightweight jacket close to me for warmth. The chilly night air penetrated into my bones, and my coughing worsened.

Then the driver spoke over his shoulder: "That's a bad cough you have, young lady."

"I know," I answered. "And I'm sorry. It has grown so much worse since I left St. Louis a couple of days ago."

"Do you have any medicine for it?" he asked.

*Matt. 5:40-41.

109

"Well, no. You see," I went on in a rush of confidence, "I just have enough money to get me to Thermopolis, where I have a summer job at a health resort. . . . I teach the rest of the year."

He gave a small laugh. "You're going to need that health place by the time you get there! Here, maybe if you chew some gum, the mint in it will help." Gratefully, I leaned over and took some.

"Thanks a lot," I replied. Maybe it did help some, but the intermittent coughing persisted. There was very little traffic on this long, winding road. Peering out the window, I felt utterly alone. A child in the rear cried in his sleep. A man's snores were interspersed with the measured whistling outlet of air through his mouth. A Spanish couple, halfway back, kept up a rapid conversation in muted tones. Once, when their voices ceased, I glanced back and saw them exchanging a long kiss. All the while, the piercing cold wrapped around me.

Our driver proceeded rather slowly into an unlit, sleepy town, looking sharply up one street and down another until he finally wheeled the big bus toward a lighted drugstore.

As we stopped, a man who must have taken this run before called out, "Hey! This ain't no stop! Whassa big idea?"

"Just keep your seats, please," answered the driver. "I won't be longer than a couple of minutes."

And he swung from the bus, disappearing into the store. General murmuring rose among the passengers, then died down as our driver—true to his word—reappeared a few minutes later. As he slid into his seat, he dropped a package into my lap.

"Here," he spoke in a low voice. "The druggist said this was the best he could do for you without a prescription."

Before I could reply, we were off into the inky night,

while the spurts of conversation of my fellow passengers gradually subsided. Then I spoke.

"That was kind of you. I'll pay you at our next stop."

"Forget it, young lady. Just take a little when the cough gets too bad. Hope it helps."

The extreme weariness, the cold, the loneliness suddenly washed over me with his thoughtful gesture, and I let the tears roll down my face as I uncapped the bottle. Then I took a long swallow of the contents, which burned my raw throat. I continued sipping away, and the cough subsided a little. Despite the coldness, I grew drowsy. I last recall curling up on the seat thinking, I'll be dead when I get there. . . . A fine specimen to appear for work at a health resort . . . I've never been so cold.

Fingers of sunlight were prying my heavy eyelids open, but I didn't want to awaken. In a half-conscious stupor, I thought I must be in heaven, because I was wonderfully warm. Then I heard the Spanish couple talking, a child's shrill "But when will we get there?" and the hum of the bus engine. I opened my eyes. There was a blue garment covering me. I realized that sometime after I had fallen asleep, our driver had eased out of his jacket so that he could spread it over a cold, sick girl. She was only another passenger in his busy world of driving, one he would probably never again see.

I never did learn that driver's name, nor did I ever see him again after we reached the end of his run. But his extension of thoughtful kindness beyond his duty has remained with me through the years as a symbol of all bus drivers, just one of our public servants we so often take for granted.

Counting My Pluses

Harold, my husband of 48½ years, developed Parkinson's and later Alzheimer's diseases. For nearly 5 years, I cared for him at home, with the help of a day-care center the last four months. When he began falling, we knew he needed to transfer into the Health Facility at Plymouth Village. Unable to stand or walk, he was lifted by hoist into a wheelchair and taken to showers, the dining room, and for short rides around the grounds.

Although confused and fearful his first six weeks in strange surroundings, Harold still greeted everyone with his famous, wide smile. He had taught young people for 43 years and worked with all ages in church choirs, and he continued to be a joyful, open channel to all. Every day found me feeding, reading, and singing to Harold, trying to ease him into his new regime. Forgetting he could no longer walk, when I'd prepare to leave in the evening, he would say, "Wait a minute, and I'll walk you home. It's dark now." That exchange continued for six weeks. Not once did I remind him he could no longer walk; I only told him he needed to stay in bed until he grew stronger. "Besides," I added, "I just walk across the street, and there are bright lights all the way home." Then he could relax.

Suddenly he no longer remembered where our home was. Despite maps and explanations, his eyes remained puzzled. When his sister and brother-in-law visited, I asked Ned to wheel him to our home; I couldn't push him up the incline. First Harold saw the lilies of the Nile, a wide swath of purple blooms in our yard, and exclaimed, "I set those out! And those roses, too!" "Do you remember when?" I asked, and he replied, "Of course, in 1979!" I was so pleased he remembered. Inside the house, he looked around, saying, "This looks like our furniture. How much do we owe on it?" To my response of "Nothing," he said, "That's good." As he looked at Ned, he said, "Will you take me to my home now? I'm tired." So, home was finally his room and bed in the Health Facility.

As time went on, he learned to know and trust the nurses and aides. When I planned a birthday party for him, I thought he would want to invite some of his Village friends. He began by naming "Marie, Pat, Sophia, and Dorothy"—all his helpers. With three shifts daily, I knew the traditional birthday cake would never do, so I asked a friend to hand print a sign that read:

"Special thanks to special care-givers
from Harold. Share my 75th birthday."

Below the sign, placed at the nurses' station, a green glass bowl held M&Ms for three days and nights, so that all his helpers had a taste of his birthday offering. Each time I wheeled him by that sign, he'd smile happily and say, "That's my party, isn't it?"

His sister, Ethel, brought bright balloons that floated above his closet, and eventually 49 greeting cards were taped to his door. On his birthday, I made him a crown, shiny with foil. K-I-N-G in black letters adorned the front. As he entered the dining room, the pianist began playing "Happy Birthday," and everyone sang, including Harold. It was all delightful, and he remembered the celebration for three days after the cards were removed.

Returning home one evening, I was greeted by dense fog. Aloud I said, "Thanks be to God I don't have to drive through that blanket to get home." That set me to counting my "pluses," and jotting them down helped offset the constant sadness in my life. Here are a few, in no particular order of importance.

113

—Many joys and sorrows that helped cement our strong marriage.

—Encouraging support from family and friends.

—A comfortable home nearby.

—My dependable car.

—We were in the right place at the right time. Amazing how God sees to our needs in advance.

—Our savings (planned for travel) were now available to augment nursing home insurance, which covered custodial care.

—Thank God I can still sing! Music reaches Harold as nothing else seems to, and often he joins in with me.

—For most of his illness, Harold knew me and most of his friends.

—And most importantly, my strong faith in a loving Heavenly Father who understands "Why," even when we cannot.

Final pluses include a Spirit who accompanied Harold into that next dimension, our love that is eternal, and a faith that whispers, "With you alway" (Matt. 28:20).

Of Living Stones

(Written the evening of Harold's death)

("The Lord is gracious . . . coming, as unto a living stone . . .
chosen of God, and precious" [1 Pet. 2:3-4].)

Like Abraham of old, Harold patiently
  Built stone upon stone throughout his life.
Harold's stones?
  Those starry-eyed children, eager to learn.
  Young men and women who were introduced to
  New facets of knowledge given them
  Diligently, quietly, with assurance.
Many young brought to him their personal problems,
  In trust, in confidence.
Large heart, long arms embraced them all
  With tender caring.
Like Abraham of old, Harold only glimpsed
  Occasional gleanings of a lifetime spent
  In faith, persistent effort with his stones.
  Those glimpses gladdened a weary heart.
Today, like Abraham of old, Harold has finally
  Moved into the Promised Land,
  His gift of earthly time expired.
Still, like Abraham of old, Harold's heritage
  Continues in his children—in *all* the
  Living stones he touched—
  "Chosen of God, and precious."
Thus, immortality.